Cecilia Mary Caddell

Hidden Saints

Life of Soeur Marie, the Workwoman of Liege

Cecilia Mary Caddell

Hidden Saints

Life of Soeur Marie, the Workwoman of Liege

ISBN/EAN: 9783337336523

Printed in Europe, USA, Canada, Australia, Japan

Cover: Foto ©Lupo / pixelio.de

More available books at **www.hansebooks.com**

HIDDEN SAINTS:

LIFE OF SŒUR MARIE,

The Workwoman of Liege,

BY THE AUTHOR OF
"WILD TIMES," "NELLIE NETTERVILLE," &c.

NEW YORK:
D. & J. SADLIER & CO., 31 BARCLAY STREET.
BOSTON:—P. H. BRADY, 149 TREMONT STREET.
MONTREAL:—COR. NOTRE DAME AND ST. FRANCIS XAVIER STS.

1870.

To

The Rev. Mother the Prioress

and the

Community of Regular Canonesses of the Order of the Holy Sepulchre,

Now Established at Newhall,

but which

flourished in Liege at the time when

" Sœur Marie "

illustrated it by her virtues,

this

𝕷𝖎𝖙𝖙𝖑𝖊 𝖂𝖔𝖗𝖐

is dedicated,

with every sentiment of affection and respect,

by

THE AUTHOR.

HIDDEN SAINTS.

SŒUR MARIE OF LIEGE.

CHAPTER I.

The kingdom of heaven, with its countless multitude of bright and exultant spirits, may be likened to a garden in which each flower is not only fair and perfect in itself, but is placed in such a manner as to give and take fresh beauty from those that are blooming round it. Some, indeed, have more, and some have less of brightness, but each has some especial virtue of its own, each has some peculiar quality by the cultivation of which it has been fashioned to perfection, and all, combined together, blend into an atmosphere of perfume and of beauty which no single class of plants, however lovely in itself, or however skillfully massed together, could possibly have produced; for the rose is never so rich in color as when embedded in green turf; and the lily never so fair as when it unfolds its alabaster blossoms against a background of shining laurels! Queens of the gardens these! We single them out from among a thousand others, and walk up to them at once, and lo! while yet we linger near them lovingly, comes a marvellous sense of sweetness on the air, and at their feet we find a cluster of blue violets sending forth so rich a fragrance from beneath their broad, green leaves, that we feel immediately as if that very scent had been needed to fill up the measure of our delight, and as if neither the rose nor the lily would have been quite so charming if some wise, cunning hand had not taught the humble little violet to blossom near them.

So it is in the kingdom of God's glory, so also is it in His Church, which may be regarded as a temporary garden, a nursery, from whence souls are daily and hourly transplanted into heaven!

Many of these blessed spirits shine so brightly by the river of life, that we are never weary of gazing on them, admiring in them the wonderful beauty of the Creator, thus reflected in His creatures. Band after band they rise before us—martyrs who by one brave act of heroic faith have carried away the crown which meaner souls weary out long years in reaching—virgins who by a more bloodless but not less generous sacrifice have won the privilege, reserved for them alone, of "following the Lamb whithersoever He goeth"—penitents who have made their lives to bleed away in the slow martyrdom of penance—confessors and doctors who have fought from morning until sundown the battles of the Church, ever boldest and thronging thickest where the fight was fiercest and the defence most full of peril—religious orders, *lastly*, and solitaries and hermits, who, like Moses, with uplifted arms and earnest supplications, have watched the battle from afar, casting in long lives of prayer and penance as their share in the glorious combat! We have in fact but to think of heaven, or to name it, and instantaneously our minds become peopled as it were with images of its beautiful inhabitants, countless in their number as the stars that gem the firmament to our human eyes, and yet each as different from the other, as if it had monopolized to itself alone all the skill and cunning of its Maker. Beautiful as they are, and countless, they are all the servants of the King of kings, and will, as we humbly hope, be our future friends and comrades in the court of heaven! The reverence, therefore, that we feel for them is naturally, and almost unconsciously to ourselves, softened by an affectionate sympathy in their victories, as well as by an humble confidence that, remembering their own past trials, they will give us aid and encouragement in the battle which we have still to fight and win before we can attain their happiness.

But while we reverence all, some we love more than others, probably because we know them better —know them, so to speak, intimately and by name! Either their office in the Church has been so high, or their life so wonderful, that every Christian eye and heart has been naturally directed towards them, or else, circumstances have let us so completely into the history of their existence, that we know, or think we know, almost all that is to be known about them. We can talk of their parentage and their position in the world, as if these were an affair of yesterday,— we can penetrate to a certain extent into the most hidden secrets of their souls,—we can tell where lay their weaknesses, and where their strength—what they had to cut away, and what to cultivate, in their natural dispositions—nay, very often we can put our finger as it were upon the one particular and especial victory; which, like a great ocean wave, carried them so far forward on the road to perfection, that afterwards they could hardly choose but to persevere until they were saints indeed in heaven.

Such were St. Ignatius, St. Francis de Sales, St. Theresa, and a hundred others; and from out of the shining ranks of these, once militant on earth, but now in heaven triumphant, we have most of us acquired the good habit of choosing some in particular, (those perhaps whose recorded tone of thought and action seems to have been most in sympathy with our disposition, or whose virtue seems strongest just where we feel that our own is weakest,) and making of them, in our desire for assistance, a bright band of heavenly brothers and protectors to aid us in our battle with the foe. It is a good and holy practice, and bears undoubtedly abundant fruit in every soul that honestly and efficaciously, and not upon the surface only, tries it; but while we thus linger lovingly upon names we know, let us not forget that there are millions of others whose names we know not—millions of blessed spirits, now bright in the gladness and glory of their God, who, while on earth, were hidden like the violet, and, like the violet, breathed out their lives in a perfume of love and prayer, known only to God and to the favored few who by the fragrance of their good deeds had accidentally discovered them.

Hidden saints they were, and none the less saints because they were unknown. Hidden saints, working ever with a quiet and persistent love at the work of their own salvation,—covering sanctity beneath the unsuspected garb of the work-day world, in which their lot in life had cast them, and gathering in, all the while, with earnest diligence, their little harvest of appointed souls, won, some to virtue by the sweet force of words and of example only, others, more violently snatched from sin by deeds of heroic penance, done secretly in the sight of God, and known to Him alone in *those* days; though, doubtless, the souls thus rescued have learned since then to *whom* they were indebted for their salvation, and will at the day of judgment testify with great joy and gratitude to the persons of their deliverers.

Few among these hidden saints have deserved better of their human brothers, few have prayed more, or suffered more, or wearied more in the search of souls, or been more successful in that search, than the poor and uneducated girl whom I have chosen for the subject of this sketch.

Uneducated I have called her, because of human wisdom she possessed but little, but that in higher wisdom, which is the wisdom of Christ crucified, she became a proficient early; and the lessons which she thus received she wrought so thoroughly into the texture of her daily life, that, while the latter is all worthy of admiration for its sanctity, it may yet, by the extreme simplicity of its ground-work, be held up as possible of imitation to numbers of pious souls whose position in the social scale is somewhat similar to her own.

She was born at Liege in the month of March of the year of our Lord 1622, and was baptized upon Easter Monday by the sweet name of Marie. It was her mother's name as well, and was given to her partly on this account, but chiefly in honor of that dear heavenly mother whose virgin maternity had commenced nearly on the same day of the month on which this child, destined hereafter to serve her faithfully in her own order of the Carmelites, entered on her earthly existence.

Her father was a saddler by trade, and according to a custom still existing in her days, his little daughter was much better known as "Marie Sellier," than by her real name of "Ock." The custom seems to have been a remnant of those yet more ancient times when, for lack of regular surnames, children received their designations from their fathers' trades—bakers, smiths, and butlers bequeathing the names of their respective occupations, (generally hereditary ones in the family,) so effectually to their descendants, that, whatever otherwise may be their rank or station now, they have remained Bakers, Smiths, and Butlers, as far as name goes, ever since.

At the time of Marie's birth, her parents were not only respectable, they were even, for their rank in life, considered wealthy; but this prosperity hardly lasted over the days of her early childhood. Trade fell off by degrees; whether from their own fault, or from circumstances over which they had no control, they grew poorer from day to day, and in their latter years were entirely supported by the industry of their eldest daughter—Elizabeth, Marie's youngest sister, having left them early to enter into the marriage state, and dying young. Marie fed their souls, indeed, as well as their bodies; refining their rough but honest natures in the religious fervor with which her own was overflowing, lifting their thoughts and their desires gradually from the things of earth to the more important things of eternity, and never relaxing or wearying in this pious toil, until death came quietly, and, with every mark of predestination in its surrounding circumstances, bore them one after the other from her arms to heaven.

There was nothing positively supernatural in the history of Marie's childhood, though there was much to foreshow her future sanctity and the nature of the vocation to which God had predestined her. Charity, the great and especial virtue of her after life, seems to have set its seal upon her from the beginning. Scarcely had she left her cradle, ere she may be said to have commenced her unconscious novitiate in those manifold works of mercy by which, years afterwards, she not only wrought out the scheme of her own sanctification as God had ruled it for her, but contrived, over and above that end, to procure the salvation of many another soul, which, but for such assistance, would almost infallibly have been lost. If she could escape for a moment from her mother's watchful supervision, she would toddle off delighted to the house of any neighbor who happened to be sick, or was otherwise infirm. There, when missed, she was certain to be found, giving what help her childish strength permitted, and comforting and consoling the poor sufferer as well as she knew how, with her baby chatter and caresses. She used often, in after life, to say that she was never really punished by her parents excepting on some of these occasions. Probably they feared contagion—an evil she was far too young to dread on her own account; and she did in fact, once, at all events, if not oftener, visit a person suffering from a disease so dangerous and catching, that her father, in order to prevent a recurrence of the action, struck her with a heavy strap, a portion of his stock in trade, and no light instrument of punishment for a creature so young and tender. The child did not confine her charities to those suffering from bodily ailments only; poverty had at least an equal, if not a larger, share than even sickness, in her compassion. No alms appeared to her too liberal, no tenderness too tender when there was question of the poor. At the beggar's very first appeal, she would rush into the house and pounce upon whatever she could find, either in the way of food or clothing, for his relief. Often, indeed, in her simplicity, and childish ignorance of the value of the article thus appropriated, she would seize upon any piece of money (gold or silver, it was all the same to her) which happened to have been left lying within reach, and carry it off in triumph to the object of her pity. This sometimes happened at moments when her parents could ill afford the loss, and they were then obliged to go themselves to the person who had so abused the simplicity of their child, and insist upon its being refunded.

Devotion to our Blessed Lady was the second note in Marie's character from whence her future sanctity might have been securely prophesied. Mary was her good mother; and she was her child, her little one, her namesake, treating with her of all that concerned the interests either of soul or body, with a childlike, innocent simplicity, which it would have been difficult indeed, if not impossible, for that good mother to have resisted. As in her charities towards the poor, so in her dealings with our Blessed Lady, the child grew extravagant the moment there was question of her service. All that she had she gave her, and when she had nothing of her own left, she sought a gift at the hands of others. The thought of Mary was with her always—if she entered a garden she brought away flowers to adorn her altar—if any one gave her toys or sweetmeats, she exchanged them at once for wax candles to burn upon it. There, among her bouquets of homely flowers, and her little poor array of tapers, Marie would spend the hours, which other children give to idle games, telling her good mother of all her hopes and fears, her wants and wishes, asking for help in her childish charities, and complaining, even as she might have complained to her human mother, of those who had either spoken to her harshly, or treated her with unkindness. Children reared in a foreign land learn its language as easily and unconsciously as they would otherwise have done their own; it is not therefore wonderful that, in such constant sweet companionship with the Queen of Heaven, Marie early became a proficient in the language of those blessed regions, acquiring a spirit of prayer, which, growing with her growing years, rendered a habitual and intimate sense of the presence of God as much a condition of her spiritual, as the air she breathed in, was of her temporal existence, In a childhood thus devoted to the worship of Mary, we naturally look for innocence, and so carefully indeed did her good heavenly mother shield her from even the shadow of temptation, that Marie not only preserved the purity of her baptismal robes unsullied, but remained as well in such an absolute ignorance of all that might most grievously have tarnished them, as is not, alas! always to be found even among children. Nor were these blessed gifts of innocence and ignorance limited alone to the age of childhood; for her confessor, who wrote her life, and who had guided her conscience for forty years, declares that although she had often to treat with notorious sinners for the purpose of reclaiming them, and though God even permitted that her own soul should be cast for a short time into the crucible of temptation, she, nevertheless, was so marvellously sheltered from all knowledge of the nature of the sin she combated, that she died at the age of sixty two, even as she had lived, *ignorant*, as well as *innocent*, as a child of five years old. And for this there was good reason! She needed no precise knowledge of sin in order to detest it! She knew that it was hateful to God, and especially opposed to the purity of Mary's heart; and this was more than enough to urge her, not merely to the most heroic efforts to snatch others from its slavery, not merely to dread and avoid its very shadow in her own person as she would have dreaded and avoided the shadow of the devil, but over and above all this, to cultivate the opposite virtue with a delicate and loving care, which soon made it bloom like a lily in the garden of her soul.

After our Blessed Lady, Marie's warmest devotion was bestowed upon St. Albert, bishop formerly, and in her time and afterwards, patron saint of Liege. His feast, which occurred on the 7th of August, was therefore kept, naturally with great solemnity, in all the churches of that city. In the church especially which Marie was most in the habit of frequenting, and which was served by fathers of the Order of Mount Carmel, it was celebrated with a devotion well calculated to strike the imagination of a child; water, blessed by contact with his relics, and considered to be of miraculous efficacy in the healing of the sick, being always distributed for that purpose among the people at close of the day's service.

St. Albert, was of course, a favorite subject for representation among the Liegois artists. Following either some local tradition, or some well authenticated incident in the history of his life, they always depict him in the company of Mary, who gives him the Divine Child with one hand, while she points with the other to a crowd of sick people kneeling in the distance, and waiting apparently for the saint to heal them. It was natural enough, therefore, that the little Marie, kneeling day after day in the Carmelite church before this picture, should have early learned to associate St. Albert in all her childish tenderness and devotion for Jesus and for Mary. She did it, too, in a very spiritual as well as touching manner, placing herself, in imagination, among the crowd of poor people whom she saw in the picture waiting to be healed, and entreating the saint by his love both for mother and for child, and by their love for him, to cleanse her soul of all its earthly stains, and to make it strong and victorious in its advance in virtue. Undoubtedly, the saint heard and granted the prayer of his innocent petitioner. Grace after grace was showered on her childhood, and most of them she attributed to her patron's intercession; at a later period of her life he treated visibly with her in all matters connected with her sanctification; more than once he protected her on occasions of great peril to the cherished virtue of her soul, and in her first serious malady, when her life was despaired of by the chief physicians of the city, she was miraculously healed by the application of his relics. To a mind under such saintly guidance, and in which the instinct of perfection was so strong already, sermons, benedictions, and catechisms seemed naturally to take the place which toys, games, and similar trifles hold in the thoughts of other children. Marie never missed them if she could help it, and she applied herself with such good-will, and her memory was so marvellously retentive, that she could still, at the age of sixty, repeat without mistake or hesitation the questions and simple hymns which she had thus learned at the age of six. This was the chiefest portion of her education, for her parents were already too poor to do more for her otherwise than to send her occasionally to a day-school. And here, again, the excessive tenderness of her heart made her suffer much, both in body and in mind. She could never see any of the little children struck, or otherwise violently treated, without showing her indignation, and even sometimes interfering in their behalf; and, as a natural consequence, the punishment from which, by her own good conduct, she was exempted, fell heavily upon her for the failings of her companions. At this humble school, and in this humble way, she soon learned to read and write, but here her secular attainments ended; and whatever afterwards she possessed of wisdom or high thought, whatever of judgment to give guidance or good counsel, whatever of eloquence to plead the cause of charity or virtue, she found them all where one of the greatest doctors of the Church declared *he* found *his* science —at the foot of the crucifix.

When Marie was about twelve years of age, her parents decided upon sending her to Antwerp, in order that she might perfect herself in the Flemish language, and obtain, besides, a more complete knowledge of the business of "*Lingere*," for which they destined her, than she could have acquired at Liege. They had a relation long settled in the former city, who was either the wife or widow of a lace merchant, or a lace merchant on her own account. This woman, who was very rich, appear to have offered of her own accord to take charge of the young Marie, promising to attach her to her own establishment; or, if that should prove impossible, to place her in some other house where she would be equally well looked after, and taught at the same time the occupation she was sent to learn.

In accepting of this proposition, the parents of Marie, therefore, no doubt, felt that they were advancing both the spiritual and temporal interests of their child by procuring her the advantages of a home where she would be guarded carefully from the dangers of the world, and where, over and above the knowledge of her own trade, she would have the chance of receiving a better education in general matters, than with their limited means, they would have been able otherwise to afford her. Marie, young as she was, comprehended at a glance all the advantages to be gained by such an arrangement, and consented willingly, and even gladly, to the separation which involved, and which, loving her parents as tenderly as from first to last she did, could hardly have been, even at that usually thoughtless age, less painful to her than to them. But Marie knew, not only that they were poorer than they had been, but that from day to day they were growing poorer; and she had already begun to realize the fact, from which her after life was to receive its peculiar coloring, that the task of supporting them would, in the end, devolve entirely upon her. There was nothing in the prospect to sadden or alarm her, for she was naturally possessed of that high moral courage, which, whatever its other modifications may be, must lie at the root of every character destined to great sanctity; and feeling that the sooner she qualified herself for the duties to which

Providence appeared to be appointing her, the better it would be both for her parents and herself, she started as soon as ever it was possible, without regret or misgiving, upon her journey. In these days of marvellous railroad facilities men can easily travel from Liege to Antwerp in the course of three or four hours; but when Marie undertook the journey, it must have occupied almost that number of days, and was, no doubt, regarded, not merely as wearisome and difficult for its duration, and the lack of regular methods of conveyance, but, like all traveling in those far-off times, as including a certain amount of risk as well. As things turned out, however, Marie's real risk appears to have begun just where it might have been supposed to have completely ended—at the gates of Antwerp. She arrived there a weary, if not a frightened, child, and after wandering uncertainly through its stately streets, which, accustomed as she had been all her lifetime to the dirt and dinginess of Liege, must have seemed a double line of palaces in her eyes, she succeeded at last in making her way to the tall and formal-looking mansion where her rich relation dwelt. She may have shrunk, poor child, a little from its show of unwonted grandeur; but she did not come as an uninvited, and had no reason therefore to suspect that she might prove an unwelcome, guest. Probably she thought, as she humbly and affectionately kissed the hand of the great lady with whom she counted cousinship, that her toil and cares at last were over, and that she had found in that proud city, in which but a few minutes before she had felt so desolate, a safe and happy home. She was destined, however, to be cruelly undeceived. There is no need to dive very deeply into the weaknesses of poor human nature, in order to discover the cause of the sudden change of conduct which ensued on the part of the woman who had promised to befriend her. "Poor people," Marie Sellier's biographer observes, with a *naiveté,* so great, that we might almost have deemed it satire, if he who uttered it had not been a good a meek religious, little likely to sting his words intentionally with venom against any of his human brothers,—" Poor people seldom find favor with their rich relations;" and so, in truth, the little Marie found it. The rich lace merchant, in sending an invitation to her Liegoise cousin, had probably imagined Marie's parents to be still in the same thriving condition in which she had known them at the epoch of their marriage;

and when, instead of the prosperous, well-cared-for-looking girl whom she had pictured to herself, there came to her door a poor, weary, lonely child, betraying, both in her present appointments and in the mode in which her journey had been accomplished, the actual lowliness of her station, she grew suddenly ashamed. She felt she could not,—no, positively! she *could* not nerve herself to the task of introducing the ragged, beggarly-looking brat who stood, with meek, imploring eyes, upon her threshold, as the relation whose expected arrival she had announced already to her proud and well-to-do acquaintances in proud and wealthy Antwerp. To cut the matter short, therefore, she flatly refused, for once and for ever, to receive her into her house. Marie must have seemed a little stunned by this unexpected rejection, for the woman added almost immediately afterwards the cheap kindness of advice; counselling her to leave Antwerp at once, and return to her own home at Liege. An ordinary girl would probably never have even attempted to appeal from this decision. In sadness or in bitterness of spirit, as the natural tendencies of her disposition prompted she would at once have retraced her footsteps, and if her after life chanced to prove unfortunate, she would, rightly or wrongly, have pointed ever to the unkindness of this first cousinly repulse as the chief cause of all her woes.

Marie was made of very different stuff, however, and took in consequence a very different line of action. Patient and smiling, and yet perfectly resolved, she waited until the great lady had poured forth her entire stock of anger and good advice upon her devoted head, and then, when it came to her own turn to speak, she announced calmly, but in a tone which left no doubt as to the reality of her intentions, her determination to remain, if not where she was, at all events in the town of Antwerp. She had come hither, she said, in obedience to her father's own commands, and for the express purpose of learning a trade, whereby to support him in his declining years, and she had no intention of departing until she had done her utmost to comply with his desires. If, in spite of all that had been said and done, her cousin should still elect to take her in, she would gladly and gratefully accept the boon of her protection; if, on the contrary, she should decline,— why, in that case, Marie would seek instruction and service in some other house, and, God aiding the undertaking, she had little doubt of ultimately finding what she sought.

Perhaps the city dame was glad to be rid of her little cousin on such easy terms; perhaps even she had soul enough to admire and appreciate the spirit of courageous independence which this resolve evinced. But if she had grace sufficient to blush for the meanness of her own conduct, she had not wherewithal to give her courage to repair it, in the *only* way in which it could have been really repaired, by receiving Marie at once into her house, and introducing her openly as a near relation. She took refuge, instead, in one of those half-measures in which spirits such as hers are fond of hiding their own weakness. As Marie *would* not leave Antwerp of her own accord, and as she could not force her, she agreed to what she could not prevent, but, instead of giving the child occupation in her own establishment, she placed her as an apprentice in that of a female friend.

This apprenticeship may be considered as the commencement of that life of suffering which was to end for Marie only with the grave—the first touch of that heavy cross which she was to bear upon her shoulders, day by day and hour by hour, until she laid it down at last at the gates of that eternal kingdom, where, like all who have borne it bravely, she would receive in exchange the crown of victory.

Her new mistress was harsh in temper, and a miser in every fibre of her ignoble being.

To save herself the expense of keeping an additional domestic, she began at once by treating Marie not merely as a servant but a slave. All the other girls apprenticed to the establishment belonged to Antwerp, and were doubtless within reach of friends who could and would see for themselves that they were not ill treated. But Marie was a stranger—alone, or something worse, her only relative a woman so evidently ashamed of her as to be little likely to interfere in her behalf, and upon Marie's young shoulders, therefore, everything hard or distasteful in the daily labors of the household, as a matter of course, was laid; her legitimate work, as "lingere" being no sooner finished, than she was turned over as a sort of nursery-maid to the children of her mistress.

These little creatures were ill fed and worse cared for, and yet she was expected to keep them in continual good humor. She was intrusted with their management, and yet she was forbidden to contradict them. She was not much older, and hardly stronger, than they were themselves, and yet she was commanded to carry them, each in turn, as often and for as long a distance as they chose to ask her. She obeyed in silence and without a murmur, but the task of dragging about heavy and unruly children at an age when she herself had almost as much need of tender carefulness as they had, and at a time, moreover, when the avarice of her mistress kept her almost starving, may have produced, and, in all probability, did produce or foster, that tendency to dropsy, from which she suffered a martyrdom all her lifetime, and of which in the end she died. She knew how to comfort herself, however, even at that tender age, for the hard cruelty of those around her, by a fuller and more generous turning of her whole eart to God; and God consoled her in return, as He will ever console those who seek their solace in Him only, by inspiring her so to adapt her daily meditations to the circumstances in which she found herself, as that the very causes of her pain became so many sources of pure joy springing up in her soul. If her chief suffering came from children, she remembered that Jesus had been once a child; and in spirit she carried *Him*, while in the body she obeyed her unruly charges, and bore them about from place to place, wherever their caprice dictated. If she felt sinking from weariness and weakness, she remembered how Mary and Joseph had carried the Divine Child by turns, and she considered how, in the journey back from Egypt, the hot sun and white glaring sands must have tried them at the very moment when (since Jesus worked no miracles on His own account or theirs) His increased weight and age had added considerably to their former trouble. So the child went in fancy from Bethlehem to Jerusalem, from Jerusalem to Egypt, and from Egypt back again to Nazareth, sweetening and sanctifying by the affections, thus produced, the weariness of duties which might otherwise have proved as much too irksome for her mental, as they undoubtedly were for her bodily, powers of endurance. She had far more difficulty in supporting the parsimony of her mistress in regard to these very children, than in anything the little creatures made her suffer themselves. They were fed, as Marie was fed herself, upon dry bread, measured out with a rigid hand, and calculated upon the iron rule of the barely necessary, nay, often even falling short of that, while to this poor fare was added, upon great occasions, an equally economical allowance of the weakest and smallest of weak small beer.

Marie, by habit, and by the fact of her ascetic tendencies, was inclined to frugality herself in all that regarded food, but she was generous and compassionate towards others, just in proportion as she was rigid towards herself; and she suffered intensely, therefore, at seeing her little charges thus stinted in their appetites. At times, in fact, these restrictions so far exceeded all measure of right and reason, that she thought herself justified in interfering; and often in after life she would describe, with a little malicious glee, the way in which she had contrived, upon such occasions, to procure some forbidden indulgence for the young objects of her solicitude.

Doubtless, she took nothing more than she considered absolutely necessary for their proper nourishment, since she, who was so tender of conscience that she shrunk from the very shadow of venial sin, seems never to have had even a scruple on this point. Indeed, the fact that what she did take, she took from the mother for the sake of that mother's children, would probably have more than justified the deed in her own mind, and in the minds of those by whom in spiritual matters she was at that time guided.

If her mistress was parsimonious in other matters, she seems at all events to have been liberal enough in blows, but these, when directed against herself, Marie bore with fortitude, and, perhaps, even with a holy joy, derived from that love of suffering and humiliation which was beginning thus early to germinate in her soul.

In her after life, however, Marie told her director, that the cruelty of her mistress was by no means the worst trial she had to undergo while residing under her roof, and that, by the grace of God and favor of His Blessed Mother and St. Albert, she had escaped from other perils far worse to contend with, than anything arising merely from hard work and personal ill-treatment. The woman, in fact, seems to have been culpably careless as to the places and persons to whom, for the sake of her wordly gains, she sent her young apprentice. On one occasion, especially, Marie was despatched with some work, which had just been finished, to the house of a gentleman belonging to the city. She was alone, and the man no sooner saw her, than closing the door of the room behind her, he addressed her in an insolent and familiar manner. By the very instinct of her innocence, Marie comprehended that his thoughts were sinful! A holy indignation for God's offended honor instantly took possession of her soul, and instead of crying out, or showing any symptoms of alarm, she stood bravely up before him, reproaching him for the baseness and wickedness of his heart with such inspired eloquence, that, rich and powerful as he was, he cowered before his childish mentor in all the cowardice and confusion of detected guilt. Marie took advantage of his astonishment to undo the door, and, without deigning to waste another word upon him, glided quietly out of the house.

Three full years she spent in the service of the hard-minded woman who could expose her to such trials, serving out her apprenticeship to its last day, and never, in all that time, even hinting, in her brief interviews with her kinswoman, at the sufferings and ill-treatment to which, in binding her to such a person, she had unwittingly consigned her.

Even without this knowledge, however, her cousin had at l: learned to recognize the noble qualities of the child whom she had treated so unworthily in the beginning ; and she tried now to make what reparation was in her power, by inviting her, the moment her apprenticeship was over, to make a stay of some months under her own roof. Marie gratefully accepted of this tardy kindness ; and, during the period of familiar intercourse which ensued, her kinswoman became so much attached to her that she did in the end, what she might with a better grace have done in the beginning,—offered her a permanent residence and position in her household.

But Marie had come to Antwerp with a fixed and settled purpose in her soul, and as she had not allowed cruelty or neglect, so neither would she suffer kindness, to divert her from its fulfilment. She loved her parents, and they required her aid; and feeling that now at last she was in a position to give it effectually to them, she declined all the flattering offers of her relative, left her comfortable and luxurious mansion, and returned, happy in her acquired talents, to her own poor home at Liege. Her cousin fortunately was too just to blame her for a decision into which the idea of duty so largely entered. She parted from her therefore kindly, keeping up an affectionate intercourse with her ever afterwards, and never failing in the "E.....nnes" or New-Year's gifts, which then, even more than now, took so important a place in the social intercourse of families.

To the last day of her life, in fact, she seems to have retained a singular love and reverence for the girl whom she had once driven, in her blind and haughty pride, as a beggar from her door; acknowledging by her conduct, at all events, if not by her words, that in thus refusing to receive Marie, she had "rejected the visit of an angel unawares."

CHAPTER III.

As Marie, between the time of her apprenticeship and the period of her after residence at her kinswoman, spent about four years at Antwerp, she must have been quite sixteen years of age when she returned to her father's house at Liege. She came back to her parents, therefore, in all the bloom and brightness of her opening youth; but instead of frittering away the hours of that golden time in idle, or worse than idle, pleasures, she took her place at once beside them, and became, what she was destined to remain to the last day of their existence, the light and gladness of their eyes and hearts, and the main support of their humble household. Marie, moreover, seems to have possessed, in an eminent degree, the art so recommended by the apostle,—she knew how to make herself "all in all to all men," in order that she might "win all to Christ." To her superiors she was ever humble and obedient; to her equals, civil and obliging; to her inferiors, who were ever the best loved because they most needed love, she was affectionate, and considerate, and overflowing with benevolence. This sweetness of character, however, never with Marie degenerated into weakness. She could be firm enough when ever the occasion called for firmness, but hers was a wise and gentle steadiness, which, avoiding all needless causes of irritation, generally succeeded in obtaining its object without offending, or at all events without irrevocably offending those in whose despite it had been exercised.

At this period of her life, says her biographer, she was very beautiful, but it was a beauty so free from affectation or self-consciousness, and so fenced about besides, and guarded by an inborn modesty of soul which made itself felt unconsciously, and without any effort on her own part, in all she said or did, that it inspired respect even more than affection in all who approached her.

Whatever Marie's personal beauty may have been, its chief charm consisted, after all, in its being united to a soul, which, still bright in the dews of its baptismal innocence, made itself visible, like light in an alabaster vase, through the fragile clay that held it, lending the soft grace of modesty to all her movements, and shedding a heavenly sweetness upon her features, such as no mere regularity of form or coloring could have conferred upon them. Long afterwards, when she had lost the first freshness of her youth, she chanced to be rapt into ecstasy in the presence of her director and of the Carmelite brother by whom he was always accompanied at such interviews, and her face assumed so strange and so sublime a beauty in that moment of unrestrained communication with her God, that the good father was seized with a sudden desire of obtaining her picture, believing that he should thus have procured for himself and his convent the likeness of a living saint. This portrait-taking has ever been a stumbling-block and a trial to the humility of the saints, and Marie only consented to sit for her likeness, when it was laid as an act of positive obedience on her conscience. Her beauty, however, was evidently rather that of expression than of feature, for a painter skilled in his art, and of high repute at Liege, failed, after many trials, in taking anything even approaching to a good likeness of her. This was done at last by a lay brother of the Carmelite order who chanced to pass through Liege, and who, knowing far less of the rules of art than the painter first employed, understood, at all events, by the instinct of his own spirituality, the nature of the expression which makes saints beautiful even in their old age; and succeeded, to a certain extent, in transferring that of Marie to the canvas.

At the period at which this picture was taken, Marie seems to have arrived at a state of almost continual ecstasy; it is not therefore wonderful that even while sitting for her portrait, Our Lord favored her with a vision of Himself. Her cousin— not the Antwerp kinswoman, but another, an inhabitant like herself of Liege, a woman of great virtue, with whom during the latter part of her life she almost continually resided—and her confessor were both present at the time, and by the beauty of her expression, and the fixity of her looks, they understood at once that something supernatural was taking place in her soul. Being desired to relate the vision (for she never spoke upon such subjects without the express command to that effect of her director,) she told them that Our Divine Lord had indeed made Himself visible to her soul, and that, after approving of her obedience in submtiting to this trial, He had desired her to tell them to place a crucifix, with a lily springing from it as from a stem, in some portion of the picture. The symbol, perhaps, had a twofold meaning. It told her that by her vow of virginity she also had dedicated body and soul to a life of suffering, and it suggested, likewise, that the virtue which the lily emblems is a flower so delicate and so easily destroyed, that it can only retain its first bloom and beauty beneath the cool shadows of the cross.

It had originally been intended to depict the sister with the book of the third order of Carmelites, to which she then belonged, in her hand; but in consequence of this vision, she was ultimately represented as holding, instead, the lily and the crucifix to her bosom, while a crown of thorns was pressed tightly on her brow.

The vow, to which this pictured lily is an allusion, Marie had taken long years before, during the lifetime of her parents. It became in fact the object of her warmest wishes almost immediately after her return from Antwerp. A vow by which the creature voluntarily makes herself body and soul the property of the Creator, seems to come, in truth, almost always as a sort of spiritual necessity to the favored few, who, like Marie, have not only preserved their innocence from childhood, but who have been fed, moreover, and stimulated to high things, by habits of mental prayer, which, commencing in her case almost from the cradle, never left her or grew cold or careless, even for an hour: increasing still in fervor and intensity, as each new day bore her onward to her grave. She was still so young, however, when she first mentioned these desires to her director, that he refused her the permission she demanded, deeming it imprudent to allow her to enter, without further and more serious reflection, upon an engagement of such a binding and irrevocable nature. Marie submitted of course to his better judgment; and she was still in this state of suspense, urged, on the one hand, by God to bind herself to Him by vow, and withheld, on the other, by obedience to her director, when Philippe Ock, her father, unconsciously precipitated matters by a project which he started for her settlement in life. The person whom he fixed upon for her future husband was a young man who worked with him at his business, and whom, in the event of his marriage with his daughter, Philippe probably intended to have taken into partnership.

The business once broached, they left Marie between them but little peace. The young man tormented her by his tender importunities; her father pained her yet more seriously by his violent reproaches. For the first time in his life, he took umbrage at her habits of devotion, telling her plainly that since he found they tended to prevent her from complying with his wishes, he would not permit her to continue them in future. He urged on her moreover, all the commonplace arguments which parents, whether rich or poor, are too frequently in the habit of employing, whenever the finger of God, seems to point out to their children any other path than the one which they in their false worldly wisdom have destined them to tread. He accused her of selfishness, because she preferred her own eternal interest to his purely temporal and human welfare —and of obstinacy and disobedience, because she listened to the voice of God speaking in her soul rather than to his own. Sometimes he told her that it was a duty which she owed to herself to make sure of her worldly position now that a good opportunity presented itself for the purpose. Sometimes he reminded her that he and her mother were growing old and would soon be dependent on her for their subsistence, hinting at the same time that devotion was not money, or likely to produce it, and that as her parents had waited and tended upon her in childhood, so now it would be her bounden duty to wait upon them, and tend them in the still more helpless and hopeless childhood of old age. These were the arguments of a coarse unspiritual nature; but though they could not shake Marie's ultimate resolution, there was enough of truth and plausibility in them to wring her soul with sorrow. It was a deep pain, almost perhaps a source of scruple to refuse her parents anything. It was the first time in her life that she had ever done so; for, up to that moment, her obedience to their slightest wishes had never either failed or faltered. She loved them moreover dearly, and had all the natural difficulty of a loving child in opposing herself to a wish which, including as it did a scheme for their future welfare, may, in all probability, have seemed as reasonable to her own mind as undoubtedly it did to theirs. But God had spoken, and she felt that at whatever cost to herself or others, He must be obeyed. He had bidden her "to incline her ear and listen;" and if He did not also tell her "to forget her people and her father's house," He gave her at least to understand most clearly that He would not permit any further or more human ties to separate her from Him.

God had spoken! And even if her director should

never permit her to make that vow, which now, more than ever, had become the object of her desires, she was yet too keenly conscious of the whispering of divine love in her soul to consider as possible for a moment the alternate of marriage.

God had spoken! But while obeying Him, she did not forget, nor did He mean her to forget her parents, and by His grace, and by the patience and gentle firmness which He enabled her to bring to the task, she succeeded at last in reconciling duties which at first sight must have seemed hopelessly opposed to each other in her mind.

To God, therefore, she pledged herself at once, to be, whether with or without a vow, entirely His own. To her father she promised all the love and duty of a loving child, and more than all the service which, as a married woman, it would have been in her power to have bestowed upon him. For she met him first upon his own ground, and spoke to him according to the human prudence of his nature. Once married, she reminded him that she would no longer be her own mistress in regard to money. Her husband would have a right to every penny she could make by work, and it was quite possible that, as time went on, he would object to her spending either his earnings or her own upon her parents. Or admitting even that he were willing to allow it, she might not be able to avail herself conscientiously of that permission. She might become a mother, in which case she would need all, and probably more than all, she could earn, for the support of her own children, while it was very certain that the cares of a family, whether large or small, would hinder her bestowing anything like personal attendence upon her parents, or assisting them by supervision in the due maintenance of their household.

After she had familiarized him for some time to such thoughts as these, Marie took a higher tone, and addressed him in the language of those purer regions of thought where her own young soul and all its hopes were centred. "If he would but trust to Providence," she said, " he would find that his trust had not been in vain. God had promised all things to those who forsook all things to find Him;" and so she doubted not that if for His dear love she refused the earthly advantages presented by this marriage, He would in some other way provide for her, not merely according to her own necessities, but over and above that measure, would give her all that was needful for the due maintenance of her parents. Living as a single woman under their protection, she would be able to work quietly and without interruption at her needle; all her earnings would go, as a matter of course, and without the subtraction of a penny, to their support, and she would be able at the same time to wait upon them and serve them herself, and to take care of their domestic concerns in a way she never could do, if any others than themselves had a claim upon her exertions.

This was both religion made practical by common sense, and common sense sanctified by religion; and old Philippe grew calm and pacified as he listened to its teachings. He gave his consent to her project; the intended marriage was no longer talked of; and relieved from all anxiety on that point, Marie gave herself up unreservedly to her feelings of innocent and holy exultation at the prospect of belonging at some time or other, however distant, entirely to God. It happened, while she was still in this frame of mind, that one of her relations married, and in obedience to her father's wishes, she not only attended the religious portion of the ceremony, but was present at the dance and other amusements by which afterwards it was celebrated.

She told her director at a later period that the

comparison which she made during that evening between the bride's future lot and her own happier fate in having been inspired and permitted to take Jesus for her only spouse, so filled up the measure of her gladness, that she danced out of the very joy of her heart as merrily as a child all night.

Innocent as was the joy and harmless the recreation, she always spoke afterwards of that wedding festival as of the one great dissipation of her life, excusing herself, however, a little on the plea that she felt she was then making her farewell to the world and its pleasures, and that a portion at least, of her exuberant spirits proceeded from that idea.

The very next day she proved the truth of her own resolution by an alteration in her dress, which, though it had alway been perfectly neat and simple, had nevertheless been similar in most respects to that of other young girls of her age and station in the world. Now, in the spirit of St. Francis de Sales, when he recommended St. Jane Frances to "lower the flag," she adopted a black dress, plain in form and of poor material; never afterwards, upon any pretext whatever, changing either, but wearing a garment of the same hue and fashion which she had chosen first, from that day until her death.

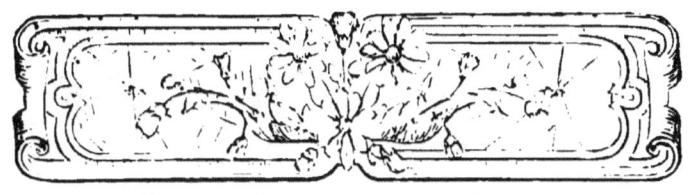

CHAPTER IV.

Having obtained her father's consent to her desire of celibacy, Marie set herself seriously to consider the best means of profiting by this permission, by making it the ground-work of a life entirely devoted to mortification and to prayer; and after long and anxious reflection on the subject, she came at last to the conclusion that she would require a more positive and enlightened rule for the purpose than any which she could make herself. She felt that she had neither sufficient wisdom, nor experience, in the spiritual life to be able to decide for herself what she was to do, and what to let alone, and she feared, moreover, with the wise humility of the saints, that without some such safe-guard, from the weaknesses and repugnances of human nature as a settled rule would give her, she might be wanting in perseverance.

Besides these reasons, Marie was quite sufficiently enlightened in the science of religion to comprehend, to the full, the advantages to be derived from some such association as she contemplated to a religious order; first, for the sake of the advice and encouragement to be thus more easily and abundantly obtained than it could be in any other manner; and lastly, and yet more stringently, on account of the principle recognized, I believe, in all communities, by means of which, the superabundance of the good works of each individual member, after having been applied to the needs of her own soul, are cast into one common treasury of merits, and become the property of all. This, of course, could have been done most completely by entering at once into religious life, but as her duty to her parents forbade her taking such a step, she was obliged to look out for some other way of accomplishing her object.

Happily the Church, like a tender and sagacious mother, had long ago foreseen the wants and wishes of such a soul as Marie's, and had provided for them by permitting and encouraging that association of seculars into orders, (popularly called third orders,) which was first established in the fullest and completest sense of the word by St. Francis Assissium.

These third orders are in reality religious orders in the midst of the world, bound by love and their own free will, rather than by vow, but having their own rules and their own superiors, and sharing in most cases in the good works and merits of the great orders from whence their rule has been taken, as the younger and poorer of the family with their elder and more wealthy brethren.

Thus, while some, called to a state of contemplation, rest in the quiet shadows of the cloister and give themselves up to the life of Mary at the feet of Jesus, others, like Martha, remain in the world, serving him as best they can, in the persons of the poor, sharing in the merits of the more perfect sacrifice of their cloistered sisters, and giving them, in return, a portion of whatever little harvest of good works they may have been enabled to gather together for themselves in the course of their active life.

The third order of the Carmelites, like the third order of St. Francis and St. Dominick, has been, in this manner and in this spirit, framed for persons who are either compelled by circumstances to remain in the world against their wishes, or who have not been called by any especial inspiration to abandon it; the original rule having been so softened down and suited to their position as to form no impediment to its other duties, while at the same time it is eminently adapted to lead them easily and swiftly to the highest degree of perfection to which, in their state of life, they are capable of attaining.

There had long been a convent of Carmelites at Liege, and under the fostering care of Pere a Corona, Marie's director in those early days, the third order of that rule had just been introduced and was becoming popular in the city. Naturally, therefore, Marie turned her eyes in that direction, though it seems probable that in any case she would have found her desires centre in an order of which our Blessed Lady was reputed the foundress and defender. "For," as the holy old Carmelite who wrote Marie's life urges, with devout and simple earnestness, "the rule of our order is especially moulded on the virtues of that ever Blessed Virgin whom St. Ambrose has proposed as a model to all virgins in all ages of the world, since, as that great saint declares, "in her, as in a mirror, you may behold the entrancing loveliness of chastity; in her as in a model, you may find all the teachings of the sublimest piety; and in her life, as in a most perfect pattern, you cannot fail, by careful study, to discover whatever is faulty or praiseworthy in your own,—what, in a word, you ought to correct, what to fly from, and what to cherish and hold fast, as the best and highest portion of yourself."

The order of the Carmelites had in fact, been hardly introduced into Liege before Marie applied to Pere a Corona for permission to join it. Being actually her confessor at the time, this father was of course well acquainted with her character, and feeling that she was already so far advanced in piety as to be likely to prove both a help and example to the other novices of the institute, he acceded at once to her request.

Marie had probably expected some opposition, for she used long afterwards to express her surprise at the facility with which her wishes had been granted, attributing it, however, not to her own merits, (true sanctity being ever unaffectedly and unconsciously blind to its own deservings,) but to the undue appreciation of them by her reverend director. But her project was destined to meet with opposition in another and less expected quarter. When Pere a Corona had given his consent to her admittance into the third order, he had coupled it with a proviso, that she should not attempt to put her wishes actually into execution before obtaining the consent and sanction of her own father to that effect. The latter, however, no sooner heard of her intentions, than he renewed all the opposition which he had made at the period when there was a question of her marriage. Having once given his consent to her desire of celibacy, it is hard to see why he should have now objected to a plan which seemed to follow, almost as a matter of course, upon the thoughts and feelings forming the groundwork of that desire. Perhaps he had hoped that her first fervor would wear away imperceptibly by contact with the world—the best possible proof, if proof were needed, that all who really desire perfection should avoid such contact. Perhaps he feared that this first public adoption of a religious calling, would lead her ultimately to leave his own house in order to seek a home in the more perfect solitude of the cloister,--whatever his thoughts may have been, he soon succeeded, hot-headed and obstinate as he was by nature, in working himself up, by brooding on them, into such a frenzy of anger and irritation as made it impossible for a time to reason with him on the subject. One day in particular, while still in this mood, he chanced to find Marie working at the white habit which she was to wear at he consecration, and feeling unable by words sufficiently to express his indignation, he snatched it out of her hand, and endeavored with all his might, to tear it into pieces.

In this dilemma, Marie had recourse to her usual arms of gentleness and prayer, and gradually, by a mingling of sweetness with judicious firmness in her intercourse with him, she succeeded in extorting his consent to her vocation.

Full of joy, she hastened at once with the good news to Pere a Corona, entreating him to fix an early day for the ceremony of her admission. It was probably upon this occasion that, while explaining to her the rules and practices to which she was about to bind herself, he chanced to mention that no member of the third order was obliged to take vows of perpetual chastity, any vow of the kind, which they chose to make, being merely understood to mean in so far as it was compatible with the state of life of the person who made it.

Marie had not patience to hear him out, but interrupting him with a mingling of holy joy and impatience in her manner, declared that, whenever she took that vow, she intended to do so in the fullest and most comprehensive meaning of the word, binding herself to its observance as strictly and as irrevocably as if her lot had been cast, in earnest and in very deed, among the cloistered sisters of the order.

In such pure and fervent dispositions as these, it is easy to imagine the loving ardor with which Marie prepared to enter upon her new state of life. She took the habit as a novice with all the usual ceremonies on the 28th of December 1644, and twelve months afterwards, Pere a Corona received her vow and public profession in the church of the Carmelites, on the last day of that year's December. Most of the professed religious, and all the members of the third order, assisted upon the occasion, the ceremony taking place before the high altar, and, as was then the custom, in presence of the Blessed Sacrament. There, upon her knees, before that celestial spouse who had so long been the object of her desires, Marie pronounced her vows,—vows which, in her case, as we have already seen, were not mere promises of milk and water only, but obligations as real and binding in their nature, as those of a cloistered nun, pledging herself to be His alone, and His forever,—in body as well as soul,—in time, not less than eternity.

This document, written by herself, was immediately afterwards deposited in the archives of the Carmelite convent at Liege, and ran as follows:

"I, Sister Marie Ock, do make my profession, and promise solemnly, obedience and chastity to Almighty God, to the ever Blessed Virgin of Mount Carmel, to the most Reverend Father General of the order of the Blessed Virgin of Mount Carmel, and to his successors, according to the rule of the third order, until death.

"Signed, on the back, in her own handwriting, in the year of our Lord, 1645."

Among the Carmelites present on this occasion, was that Pere Albert de St. Germain who afterwards wrote her life, and whom God had destined for the conduct of Marie's soul, during the last forty years of her existence. He was at that time quite a young man, and being only in the fifth year of his own profession, could not, of course, have foreseen the close spiritual connection which was hereafter to exist between them. Nevertheless, he tells us, that he was exceedingly struck by the fervor and resolution with which she pronounced her vows, and though he had never before seen her, or even heard her name, and though he knew nothing whatever of the virtue by which even at that time she was distinguished above her fellows, he felt at once, that she was actuated and filled by the spirit of God to a degree which he had never observed before in any profession at which he had assisted.

Marie's fervor and resolution would in fact have carried her much farther than the mere observance of the rule to which she had thus publicly declared her adhesion. Gladly and joyfully would she have engaged herself instead, to the more austere life of a cloistered Carmelite; and probably at that time she hoped that, sooner or later, she would have been enabled to do so. For the present, however, her duty to her parents forbade the step; and she was forced to content her zeal by binding herself instead, not only to the most scrupulous exactness in the lesser engagements which she had just contracted, but by making, over and above that engagement, a firm resolution to become, in all but the fact of inclosure, a true Carmelite—by the observance in the strictest sense of the word both of the spirit and letter of the rule. How she kept this resolution, the history of her life will tell! So effectually, indeed, did she carry out her own idea that, albeit not bound as a secular to such strict observance, she never omitted anything she could do,—

praying, fasting, and suffering in the measure, and above it, of her cloistered sisters,—as obedient as the most scrupulous among them to superiors, and as observant of the rules—of the smallest as well as of the more important—regarding each of them as a separate rung in that ladder which the blessed Angele, a nun of the order, had seen in a vision, and by mounting which, as an interior voice assured her, all faithful Carmelites would in the end reach heaven.

Once admitted to her profession, Marie applied herself more than ever to prayer and mortification; and though in the latter particular she was so severe that her director was often compelled to interpose his authority, in order to compel her by obedience to more mercifulness towards her body, her exterior life continued to be so calm and simply regulated, that it presented nothing remarkable on the surface, and that none but the very few admitted to her confidence were aware of the deeds of heroic sanctity which lay beneath. For God alone and in God she lived, and the higher portion of her life was hidden, as she desired, with Him. Externally her life was one of labor. No fervor of prayer, no excess of mortification was ever suffered to interfere with her duty to her parents, or the unremitting toil by which she earned their daily bread, so that men at first merely regarded her as a good and well-conducted young person, exceedingly devoted to her parents, and rather more pious, perhaps, than was usual at her age and in her state of life.

She rose at four, went straight to the church, heard Mass, and afterwards made an hour's meditation. She then returned to the house; and after having set everything in order for the day, sat down to her work in company with two or three young girls, whom she was soon enabled by her industry and reputation for skill at the needle to receive as apprentices. She chose these girls less for their aptitude to learn than for the need which they had of religious training and protection, making their apprenticeship a reason and an excuse for bringing them to reside entirely in her house and under her own eye, until such a time as she judged them to be competent to take care of themselves.

It would be hard to say how many young creatures she thus snatched from the woes into which poverty, or the weakness of the frail, human nature in them, was about to plunge them; and once she had taken their charge upon her soul, she never allowed either the threats or calumnies, or even the severe personal ill-treatment, to which she was sometimes subjected by those whom she had thus balked in their wicked designs, to terrify her into abandoning them. Naturally she took even greater care of their spiritual concerns, than of the temporal training by which she proposed to enable them to work honestly thereafter for their own subsistence. Over and above the force of her own example, and of her affectionate advice and exhortations, she wisely tried to give new interest to their work by reading aloud; the lives of saints and other books of the same kind, calculated at once to instruct and amuse them, being chosen for the purpose. Mindful at the same time of the sanctification of those still dearer to her heart by the ties of nature, she managed to arrange these lectures so that her old parents could always be present at them; and, as happens often enough in such cases, by dint of hearing thus continually of the deeds of the saints, these good folk, who had passed the greater portion of their lives as merely ordinary good Christians, ended by becoming very saintly and heroic ones before they died.

Work being terminated at mid-day, the little party took their meal chiefly together. Marie, however, generally set aside her own share for the poor, satisfying her appetite with bits of broken bread and a cheap and unsavory sort of cheese, which she took while smiling and conversing with the others, eating with as much apparent zest as if she had reserved for herself the daintiest and most appetising portion of the repast. Dinner over, she retired to a small chamber, which she had appropriated for the purpose of quiet prayer, and there made another hour of meditation, accompanied by examination of conscience, the latter exercise being repeated at intervals during the course of the day. The afternoon, after she had distributed their second task of work among her apprentices, was devoted entirely (especially during the last years of her life) to works of external charity—to visiting the poor, the sick—those who were in prison for a period, or who were condemned to die—and lastly, and more than all the rest, to seeking out and consoling those poor creatures, whom, either by interior illumination on the part of God, or by some exterior circumstance which had come accidentally to her knowledge, she knew to be in danger of the suicide of their own souls by sin.

This was the distribution of her time upon week days, but Sundays and holidays of obligation were spent almost entirely in the churches, a large portion of those hours of quiet and recollection being most usefully devoted to a review of the manner in which she had fulfilled her obligations during the preceding week. Possibly it was owing to this very practice that she was enabled so to manage matters as to combine religion with her daily duties in such a way that the one never interfered with the other, and that her devotion, excessive as it was, was burthensome to no one. Over and above an amount of prayer which seems incompatible with the time given to good works, and of good works which seem equally incompatible with a life of almost constant prayer, Marie contrived to keep her father's house in order; to secure to him and her mother a decent maintenance; to instruct her apprentices, and to watch over their spiritual training; to educate her niece, whom she had adopted on the death of the child's mother, her younger sister, and to furnish her ultimately with fortune sufficient to establish her respectably in the marriage state; and she managed, besides, to give abundant alms to all who had need of her assistance. This looks almost like a miracle, and yet it was not!

Marie contrived to do more than an ordinary

good person, because she had more than an ordinary good person's appreciation of the value of time. Like the saints, she considered that each moment, as it passed her, should be sent forward freighted with golden treasures for eternity, and none, therefore, were wasted either in idleness or pleasure. This was, in fact, the true secret of the saints, and the cause why each of them in their degree accomplished such a multitude of good works as seem, humanly speaking, impossible in the short term of years to which man's life is limited. It was *their* secret, but it might be also *ours* if we chose to take it; and if we would but do so, and act honestly upon it, there would, I think, be fewer complaints than there are unhappily at present, as to the incompatibility of prayer with the duties of the active life. Moreover, in thus giving its due preponderance to the spiritual element in our existence, we should soon discover a fact, of which some of us seem hardly sufficiently aware at present, namely, that Christ meant really what He said, and said no more than He really meant, exhorting His followers "to seek first the kingdom of God and His justice," He added this especial promise—" and all other things shall be added to you."

CHAPTER V.

Besides her daily and weekly exercises of devotion, Marie contrived every year to make a spiritual retreat of ten days, during which time she applied herself entirely to the examination of the state of her soul, and of the progress she had made in virtue. For this purpose she generally chose that part of the twelve months in which a good many festivals of obligation occur nearly at the same time, partly, perhaps, for the kindling anew of her devotion towards the mysteries thus commemorated, but chiefly, probably, from a wise wish to conciliate her religious with her temporal duties, by giving to the former those days which, in any case, she would have been prevented by the discipline of the Church from bestowing on the latter.

She had the good habit also of writing down the results of these retreats, and of giving an account of the meditations in which they had been employed, marking out not only the faults which she had discovered in the course of her self-examination, but the particular virtue, also, by which each individual failing was to be combated and overcome.

Many of these little pamphlets fell, either during her life-time, or afterwards, into the hands of her director, and he gives us a sample of them, in order, as he says, to show his readers her faithfulness in prayer, and the care which she took to draw from it its full fruit for the guidance of her soul. He might have most justly added, also, in order to show how the saints grow in humility, as they grow in love; and how the most trivial faults, the most accidental omissions, which appear, alas! as mere nothings in the eyes of an ordinary Christian, become, to a soul enlightened by the gift of prayer, evils of great magnitude, to be regarded seriously and vigorously combated, as obstacles to the loving kindness of its God.

I give them as he did, without change and without important retrenchment, for I think we may learn more for the conduct of our own souls by a minute acquaintance with the interior dispositions of the saints and of the way they took in the pursuit of virtue than by a history of their visions and miracles, as we can never too seriously remember, the latter being by no means the *cause* of their sanctity but simply its *result!*

She commences then the sketch of her interior dispositions in these words:—

"I dedicate all my meditations to the honor of God and of the Blessed Virgin, intending them for my own conversion, and to produce a complete reformation in my way of life; and in order to accomplish this last most perfectly, I promise—

1st. "Faithful obedience to God's inspirations, for I perceive that all the disorders of my past life have proceeded from want of due correspondence to His graces.

2d. "God in His goodness has given me grace to understand, during this retreat, the little care or value which I have hitherto set upon my own soul, preferring, as I have so often done, vain amusements and bodily comfort to its advance in virtue; I promise, therefore, so to order my life in future, that the soul shall command as mistress, and the body as a servant shall obey; and for this purpose, I resolve to punish the latter continually, and to mortify it in everything, and on every occasion as much as I can, and as much as its strength will let me.

3d. "I will attach myself to nothing, and will desire

nothing for the future but the love of God and my own advance in virtue.

4th. "God has made me comprehend at last, that the greatest obstacle to my perfection lies in fear of the constant mortification by which alone it can be attained; I promise, therefore, to let no day henceforth pass without reflecting, once at least in the course of it, seriously upon the great debt I already owe Him, and I will regard, moreover, that day as lost in which I have not suffered something.

5th. "I find I have lost the habit of preparing myself for prayer, and this has caused me in some measure to neglect it; I promise God, therefore, never again to present myself to His divine majesty for the purpose of prayer without having carefully and seriously prepared myself for it.

6th. "I perceive a tendency in my disposition to act without the advice of my director; I promise therefore, for the future to undertake nothing, little or great, without asking his express permission.

7th. "I have an undue love and desire for the possession of anything I see which is curious or beautiful; I resolve, therefore, never to have anything for my own use which is not perfectly plain and common.

8th. "God has given me to comprehend, on the

one hand, the small esteem which I have for my vocation, and on the other, the great favor and mercy which He has shown me in bestowing it upon me; I promise therefore, in order more perfectly to cherish and preserve it, to detach myself entirely from creatures, to consider even the least of my actions as a means of pleasing Him, and consequently as a matter of great importance, and never to allow a day to pass, without reflecting, once at least in the course of it, with great love and gratitude, upon His goodness in allowing me thus to dedicate myself to His service.

9th. "I have been hitherto continually wanting in zeal, tepid and lazy in the service of my God; now I promise, with His helping grace, to be really fervent for the future, and never to allow myself truce or rest in working for Him.

10th. "I perceive that my natural affections are quick and inclined to be immoderate, and that my thoughts are low and earthly; I promise, therefore, to repress, bridle, and mortify my affections in every way, whenever they lead towards creatures, and to keep my eyes and thoughts henceforth fixed on heaven, never lowering them again to the things of earth.

11th. "I have been full of self-love and self-esteem, and unable to endure reprimand; now I promise to consider blame, whether just or unjust, as the most precious favor which God can send me through His creatures.

12th. "I have been obstinate and unwilling to obey, but I promise for the future to be docile and obedient in all things.

13th. "I have been impatient and troublesome to every one about me; in all these matters I will mortify my own will and temper for the future.

14th. "I have been too fond of my own opinions, defending them with warmth, and despising those of others; I promise now always to suspect my own as having their origin in the promptings of self-love, and to embrace those of other people as heartily as if the very truth itself were in them.

15th. "Not having hitherto thought much of death, and considering that this may in part be the cause of my indolence, and of the too great liberty which I give my senses, I resolve in future to meditate, every now and then, seriously upon it, as being a consideration most needful to salvation.

16th. "Self-love has always made me unwilling to acknowledge my faults; I promise, therefore, to seek in future every occasion openly to accuse myself of them. Also, I will be more obedient to the exhortations of my confessor—more constant at sermons, and more attentive to good inspirations—more careful, in fine, to imitate the virtues of the saints, remembering that all who have taught me, whether by word of mouth or by example, will on the day of judgment, be my accusers or excusers before God.

17th. "Self-will is the fuel of hell, which St. Bernard tells us would not exist without it; I resolve, therefore, most earnestly, to crush and mortify it in the least as well as in more important things.

18th. "As charity, on the other hand, is one of the greatest joys of heaven, and as we cannot hope to possess it *there* without having first tried at least its practice *here*, I promise never to omit anything by which I can innocently serve or please my fellow-creatures, and to abstain, even at my own expense, from all that might sadden or displease them.

19th. "I have hitherto confessed by habit, with little contrition or purpose of amendment, but I resolve for the future never to confess without great and diligent preparation, and positive resolutions as to the avoidance of sin.

20th. "I perceive that, owing to my want of habits of mortification, the smallest pain makes virtue difficult, and the merest trifle is sufficient to amuse and distract me from its pursuit; also, and for the same reason, the smallest contradiction troubles me, the smallest reprimand disheartens me, the least advice annoys, the slightest success puffs me up, and the smallest reverse utterly disheartens me; in one word, I have sought myself everywhere and in everything that I have said or done; now, therefore, I promise God that, by His grace, I will never allow myself to pause or be discouraged, that I will never slacken in my efforts, that I will absolutely decline in future all temporal amusements and relaxations which are nothing in themselves, and which lead to nothing ; and that always and everywhere, in adversity as in prosperity, I will look to God, and God alone, seeking His honor and glory in all that I say or do, without any regard to my own interests in the matter.

21st. "I have hitherto too much neglected the reading of pious books; therefore I resolve for the future never to allow a day to pass without a lecture of the kind.

22d. "I will perform no action, however insignificant, without having first offered it to God, and I will thank Him upon its completion.

23d. "I will observe a modest reserve in all that I say, and in all my actions.

Lastly. "I will bear in mind, and continually remember, that these resolutions, written by my own hand, will be put in evidence against me on the day of judgment. They will be the test of my fidelity, and by them I must stand or fall."

With these resolutions, Sœur Marie Albert—for, on the day of her profession, she had taken the latter name in honor of her great patron—commenced her religious life. The sequel of that life will show how faithfully she corresponded to them, never either faltering or failing in them, for a moment, never lessening or relaxing, but rather increasing her efforts as years went by, and the whisperings of God's Holy Spirit in her soul kept prompting her to higher things; until she reached at last the full measure of that sanctity to which He had predestined her, and which probably the saints never absolutely attain to, until the moment, when ripe for heaven, He recalls them to Himself.

In reading this history of her retreat, it must be borne in mind, moreover, that whether in speaking of her actual failings, or of the tendencies to failings which she observed in her own character, Marie fell into those habits of holy exaggeration which are a peculiarity of the saints, whenever they touch upon their sins. Meaner spirits either palliate their faults from pride, or by reason of the hardness of the hearts within them, cannot, even when they would, form a full and perfect appreciation of their malice. The saints, on the contrary, who read their souls by the light of God's bright presence ever shining in them, behold such ingratitude and such a wanton waste of the precious blood of Christ in the slightest of their faults, that they are filled with sorrow and confusion whenever they turn their eyes inwards on themselves, mourning over failings which an ordinary Christian would hardly even think of carrying with him to the tribunal of confession, as so many blows dealt insolently to the majesty of God, and so many treasons to His goodness.

Thus Marie had led from her cradle a life of innocence and prayer; and yet she speaks of the "disorders" of her past life, a term which, in the mouth of an ordinary Christian, would have meant something very different from the venial failings into which even the purest and most pious persons must, by reason of the weakness of their human nature, occasionally fall. She hints at dissipations and vain amusements, yet her existence was one of unceasing toil, and the one great dissipation of her life seems to have been that wedding dance at which, partly to please and gratify her father, she was present in her early youth. She speaks of her self-will and disinclination to ask advice, and yet she never did anything, even of small importance in itself, without having first consulted her director on the subject. She mourns over her self-love and disobedience, and yet she lived with her parents, as submissive to them as if she had been still a little child, until she had long passed her own youth, and was herself declining to old age. She says she was tenacious of her own opinions, and her director tells us that in fact her judgment was so superior, and so evidently under the guidance of God's Spirit that it must have been an act of heroic virtue in her to renounce, as she had promised, and as she ever afterwards did most perfectly, her own for the opinions of less gifted persons. Lastly, she speaks of her fear of pain and dislike to mortification, and yet she had inured herself to both from childhood; and dating from the hour on which she had resolved to consider the day lost in which she had not performed some positive act of penance, her director very positively assures us that she never, in that sense, lost any.

And these penances were no mere child's play! She wore chains and a hair shirt night and day, the hair shirt being not simply a belt or tunic, but a garment long enough to cover her whole person, with sleeves ending only at the wrist; and the chains being furnished with sharp points placed in such a way as to pierce deeply into the flesh. Her disciplines also were made of chains, and as if this were not enough, she strewed her poor bed with thorns, and even introduced them into her dress and hair. Her fasts were rigorous and frequent. She often passed the entire day without eating, and at all times her food was scanty in quantity, and, as we have already seen, anything but appetising in its quality. She never touched fruit, the only luxury of the poor in the warm summer weather; never smelt at flowers; never looked at curious or pretty things; never, if she could help it, listened to sweet sounds! Her body was a garment in which she lived, because it had been so ordained, but which she was resolved should in no way whatever minister to her delight until she should again clothe herself with it at the universal resurrection, in order to feed among the lilies in the garden of her Divine Spouse. More than all the rest, she mortified her own will and judgment, so that in her, the spirit of penance extended, as it ever does, when it is genuine, from the outer to the inner life, from the chastisement of the flesh to the far more perfect, because more hidden and more humiliating to human pride, crucifixion of the spirit.

She was only twenty-six years of age when Pere Albert first took charge of her soul, and he found her already far advanced in this life of penance, which she had so contrived to systematise, as that night should yield her sufferings as well as day. As a prudent director, he felt himself called upon to interfere, and to protect her against herself. He did not, of course, forbid her mortifications, but he assigned her certain days for certain penances, and fixed some limit to their duration. Nevertheless, he tells us that whenever there was any great deed of charity to be done, a sinner to be converted, or a soul to be relieved from the flames of purgatory, he felt himself bound in conscience to loosen the reins, and to leave her for a time to the promptings of her charity; reserving, however, always to himself the right to step in and interfere whenever he thought she was exceeding the limits of her strength. But whether he diminished her penances or increased them, he found her ever as submissive and docile as a child, and it was by this, the safest of all tests, the test of obedience, that he tried the truth of her other virtues. So long as she yielded readily in matters in which souls less perfect find ever the most difficulty in obeying their directors, he was content to let God work out His own designs in this chosen soul, confining himself to watching carefully each indication of His divine pleasure, and guiding her by the light which he thus received, safely and swiftly in the path of heroic sanctity she was so evidently called upon to tread.

CHAPTER VI.

On the day of her profession, Marie, as we have already seen, gave herself body and soul to God; it now only remains to ask what God, in accepting of this holocaust of love, chose to give in return to her. The answer may seem strange to worldlings, but it will be nothing new to those who have studied God's thoughts and ways in His dealings with His loved ones. For albeit He gave her nothing that, according to the opinion of the world, could have been esteemed desirable; He gave her, for all that, the most precious gift that, omnipotent as He is, it is in His power to bestow upon His creatures. He gave her what He gives ever to His saints in the days of their fleshly existence—what He gave to the mother of His only Son—what He gave to that Son Himself —a cross, heavy enough to tax all her powers of endurance, and which she was to bear day after day without truce or rest up the Calvary of this mortal life, until that last final hour when He Himself should bid her lay down upon it, even as His Divine Son had lain down already, and die upon its arms.

At the moment of her consecration to religious life, Marie had promised not merely to afflict her body for God's sake, a thing common enough among fervent Christians, but she had offered it up to Him in order that it might be consumed wholly and entirely, even as were consumed the holocausts of the old law, by sufferings in His service.

And in the most real and literal reading of the word, that offer was accepted! God deigned to co-operate with His creature in this whole burnt-offering which she wished to make Him of herself; and while she afflicted her body with hair shirt, and scourge, and daily fast, and nightly meditation, until her confessor was obliged in common prudence to interfere, to prevent absolute destruction of the frail tenement she was tormenting, her divine Spouse did His own share in the work by sending her the involuntary, and perhaps therefore, in His eyes, (because where the will is, there is always cause at least for suspicion,) the more meritorious suffering of disease. He did even more than this, for to the pangs of illness He added its "*abjection,*" that "*abjection*" of which St. Francis de Sales speaks so touchingly, and commends so wisely, as the greatest possible sanctifier of pain, the last finishing touch, as it were, from the hand of God, when He mercifully means to give the sufferer the full merit of his trial by purifying him from that secret pride, which (such is the corruption of our poor fallen nature) even the consciousness of patient suffering might otherwise have engendered. Her principal malady, the one from which she suffered all her lifetime, and of which at last she died, was dropsy, a disease, which, by the strange alteration it produces in the figure, gave the key-note to a thousand foul-mouthed calumnies from those who loved her not. It may seem strange enough at first sight that one so innocent in her life, and so obscure—so harmlessly, and yet so usefully, employed—should have attracted enemies; but no word that Christ ever uttered has been falsified in the result; what was true in the beginning will be true even to the end, and when He said, "The world hath hated them, because they are not of the world," He said it, not of the disciples only, who were then actually in His presence, but of all, who to the end of time will, in spite of the world's sneering and ill usage, dare to gather round His standard.

Marie was not of the world, but being of humble

station, it would perhaps have passed her over in contemptuous silence, if she had not, by the very character of her vocation, interfered with its sinful pleasure. Many indeed loved her, and were edified by her virtues; but many, on the other hand, felt that her life was a reproach to theirs, and hated her for the silent lesson; while, with many more, she came into still closer contact, and by withdrawing the poor objects of their sinful attachments from their grasp, earned their undying hatred. To such as these last, the peculiar appearance of her malady afforded a subject of fiendish exultation and a source of calumny which never failed them, cropping up more or less vigorously every now and then, whenever she had succeeded by her heroic charity in thwarting their evil wishes.

Marie felt these calumnies most acutely—how indeed was it possible that she could do otherwise? The brighter the sunshine, the deeper seems the shadow! The more perfect the purity of the mind, the more thoroughly it comprehends the deep injury done to it by imputations against its purity!

Marie had no dearer wish than that her life should waste and wear itself away, like the lamp which burns before the sanctuary, until it expires at last, from the simple lack of oil wherewith to feed on! Suffering, therefore, she sought and longed for, and pain and sickness of the body she welcomed as a sure and speedy means of saving her own soul and the souls of others. But this calumny against a virtue, which, with the sure instinct of the saints, she had cherished almost without knowing wherefore, from her cradle was indeed abjection!—abjection so deeply, terribly humiliating to her pure soul, (in love as it was with the purity of the angels,) that it sometimes had power to cause the cup of bitterness to flow over, and once at least in her lifetime forced her to break silence and to cry out, even as her Divine Spouse, shame-crushed and broken-hearted in the garden of Gethsemane, had cried out before her, for the withdrawal of the chalice.

This "once" happened on the feast of St. Aloysius, who had ever been one of her most chosen patrons. She was already very ill, and feeling that the attack would be a severe one, she addressed herself to him, ingenuously complaining of her Divine Spouse, who, not content with afflicting her with the malady itself, exposed her, as its necessary consequences, to the evil-minded suspicions of the world. The saint appeared to her at once and healed her, but even as he did so, he reminded her that, as she had given herself entirely to God, so she was bound to leave herself entirely in His hands, not drawing back or seeking to reclaim the offering she had made, but abandoning herself, body and soul and human reputation, to His loving care, certain that whether He left her to honor or to dishonor, to sickness or to health, He was still caring for her truest interests, and promoting them in the way in which He, as God, foresaw they would be most speedily and securely promoted for eternity. Another time, when she was ill, and haunted, probably, by somewhat similar feelings of shame and sorrow, her Divine Spouse Himself deigned to visit her, consoling her in these tender and touching words, which should move the hearts of all who are destined to a life of suffering to very especial sentiments of love and joy: "Know, daughter," it was thus He spoke, "that when you are well and serve Me by active works, I embrace you with My right arm, but when you are suffering and unable to do aught but patiently to suffer for Me, then I embrace you with My left, so drawing you nearer and closer still, until you repose upon My very heart!"

Marie's first attack of dropsy occurred six years after she had taken the habit of a religious, and brought her nearly to death's door. The physicians, in fact, had quite given her over, when, having made a novena to her great patron St. Albert, she was cured almost instantaneously after drinking some water which had been touched by his relics. The miracle was known to all, and having been publicly examined into and attested by the authorities, both civil and religious of the town, Marie hung up a votive tablet in the Carmelite Church to commemorate her cure. Pere Albert had just at that time assumed direction of her soul, an office which he seems to have fulfilled with consummate skill and prudence, and which he continued to hold during the last forty years of her existence. In describing her miraculous cure upon this occasion, he tells us, that she enjoyed for a few years afterwards a certain amount of health, interrupted indeed often enough by illness, sometimes of many months' duration, but still leaving a large margin of time during which she was able to work vigorously and unceasingly in the service of souls. Pere Albert seems to have convinced himself by very positive experiments, that albeit her maladies presented all the appearances of natural disease, they did not arise in reality from natural causes, seeing that the remedies which would have been efficient in any other case, instead of curing, or at all events of checking, actually with her increased disease. This fact he tested, as did also one or two very enlightened Jesuits to whom, in his occasional absences from Liege, he made her address herself, by every possible proof it was in his power to apply, sometimes forbidding her to make novenas, at others forcing her to persist in natural remedies, though she visibly grew worse beneath them, and never allowing her to leave them off until there seemed positive danger to her life in insisting upon this course. Marie herself was quite aware that hers was no case for doctors, but though she often said so, and begged to be allowed to leave off their treatment, she continued to follow it without a murmur, waiting, heroically obedient to the last until the precise moment when her director, of his own accord, should allow her to intermit it. No sooner, however, was this permission given than she turned instinctively to Our Blessed Lady and St. Albert, entreating their assistance, and her confidence was usually justified by a speedy cure. Most frequently this result was obtained by application of the relics of St. Albert, and presented all the usual indications of a miracle, being sudden and complete, and unaccompanied by any such intermediate period of convalescence as would have been the inevitable consequences of a natural recovery. She passed at once from death to life, from a state of utter prostration, the consequence of months of suffering, to one of vigor and strength sufficient to allow of her returning immediately to the duties of her station, so that neither the doctors who had previously attended her, or the numerous visitors who had seen her during her illness, could doubt for a moment that this renewal of perfect health was an especial gift of God, accorded to her through the intercession of His Blessed Mother and His saints, and as the reward of her own faith and patience.

The miraculous cure wrought upon her body during her first great illness, produced an almost equally miraculous effect upon the soul of her own father. The man does not seem to have been vicious, or irreligious, in the broad sense of the word. He was simply ignorant and gross-minded, and therefore incapable of distinguishing between the spiritual and merely human elements in his own existence, or of appreciating them at their relative value. His daughter's holy life, accompanied as it was by the most childlike obedience to his wishes, had no doubt been leading him gradually and unconsciously to a more refined and spiritual way of thinking; but it was not until a visible miracle, wrought on her behalf, had set the seal, as it were, of heavenly approbation on her vocation that he saw it in its true light.

He surrendered himself generously and at once to his new convictions, and became changed into another man. The companions in whom he had formerly delighted no longer pleased him. Heaven and heavenly things seemed alone worthy of his consideration, and the time which he had been used to spend in very different society, he now devoted to discoursing with his saintly child upon the best means of securing his salvation.

Day after day he might be seen with her assisting at the Mass, which one of the Carmelite fathers said at dawn; and Sundays and holidays he now spent, as she did, almost entirely in the church. Under her advice and guidance also, he began to approach the Sacraments more regularly and frequently than before, and became constant in his attendance at public catechisms and sermons. Three or four years were spent in this new way of life, and then, only a day or two after he had approached the Sacraments, he was struck down by apoplexy, the priest having just time to administer Extreme Unction before he died in his daughter's arms. Marie afterwards learned by supernatural communication that he had died in a good state, and been accepted, a happiness which he no doubt owed in a great measure, if not entirely, to the prayers and merits of his daughter. He had been poor and struggling for many years before this occurred, and died considerably in debt. Probably he was a bad manager, as well as an unsuccessful artisan; for his liabilities, though not heavy in themselves, were large for a man in his position, consisting of a number of small debts, incurred very likely here and there, and from time to time, without much thought as to how they were ultimately to be repaid, until they amounted at last to something over two thousand five hundred francs —that is to say, to a hundred pounds in English money. He left nothing to meet this debt but some furniture of little value, and the utensils of his trade, which, even if sold at their highest price, would have been totally inadequate for the purpose. By the law of the country, as it then was constituted,

Marie might either have accepted this inheritance, in which case she made herself liable for every debt that could be proved against it, or she might have refused it, and thus have escaped altogether the penalty of payment. There were no lack of worldly-minded friends to advise her to the latter course, but Marie had other and nobler thoughts on the subject. She considered that the payment of just debts would be the highest act of piety which, as a child, she could render to her parent; in a human point of view, because it freed his memory from all charge of dishonesty or injustice, and, in a spiritual, because perhaps he was suffering still in the flames of purgatory for his nonfulfilment of that duty in his lifetime.

She told her advisers, therefore, that her father's debts were obligations which he had voluntarily contracted, and which he had had every intention of satisfying the moment his means permitted. Since, however, previous misfortunes and sudden death had deprived him of the power of satisfying this obligation in his own person, it was her bounden duty, as his daughter, to stand in the gap and fulfil it in his stead, and she was resolved accordingly to do so. And as she said, so indeed she did, bravely, constantly—and in the end, successfully. People blamed her then—as they would blame her now; and called her then—as they would call her now—rash, silly, obstinate, and foolishly regardless of her mother's interest and her own. Marie would not even listen to them. She threw herself generously into the arms of Providence, and Providence generously answered the appeal. Her creditors themselves admired her probity and gave her time; and by dint of working double tides, by day and night, she succeeded at last, not only in acquitting her father's obligations, but in obtaining also for his soul all those extra offices of devotion which she would have been expected to have procured for him, if the inheritance which he had left her had been other than his debts. He was honorably interred at her own expense in the church of the Carmelites, before the altar of St. Albert, to whom, after the miraculous cure of his daughter, he naturally felt an especial devotion, and underneath the very spot where he had been in the habit of hearing with her the Mass of dawn. Besides the solemn office and dirge usual on such occasions, Marie had also private masses and novenas continually offered up for the repose of his soul, her own prayers and bodily macerations being no doubt increased in measure and intensity, and thrown into the scale for the same intention.

After her father's death, her mother naturally became more than ever the object of her loving care. She survived her husband only six years, and then she also lay down to die. Her malady, though pronounced mortal from the beginning, was nevertheless lingering in its character, and thus she had time mercifully given to her to become a saint upon her death-bed. In the hands of her holy daughter, and under the teachings of great suffering, she attained at length, as Pere Albert, who attended her in her last hours, tells us, to such sublime sentiments of the love of God and desire of beholding Him, as in the natural order of things could only have been expected from a soul long used to the highest prayer of union with Him, and she died at last, as her husband had died before her, calmly and happily in the arms of her child. Scarcely had she passed out of this world, ere Marie and many others who were with her at the time received a supernatural intimation of her happy state. For, while Marie who loved her most affectionately was weeping bitterly beside the death-bed, a voice coming most distinctly from the white and motionless lips of her dead mother spoke thus—reproaching her, as it might be, tenderly with the selfishness of her sorrow, "Why do you weep my happiness?—know that I am in glory?" This voice was heard distinctly, not by Marie alone, but by her cousin and many other persons who were praying with her at the time. Pere Albert was instantly informed of the occurrence, but though he tells us, that in consequence of what he had himself observed in the soul of this poor woman during her illness, he could easily believe it, he nevertheless acted in the matter with the prudence which seems most especially to have distinguished him, neither denying nor affirming, but causing masses to be said and prayers to be offered up as usual for the departed soul, knowing full well that if, as he hoped, she no longer needed them, God would accept them as spiritual alms for the relief of some other poor sufferer in the flames of purgatory.

In the course of the next two years Marie lost the last of the fireside group of her childhood in the person of her sister Elizabeth. This poor woman seems to have been anything but fortunate in her married life. It almost appears as if she had been ill-treated by her husband, and with the exception of one little girl, who was about four years of age at the period of her own death, she had had the additional misery of losing all her children one after another almost as soon as they were born. She died nine days after giving birth to an infant, who was either dead beforehand, or who did not survive her. Up to the very day of her death, however, she had been doing so well, that her sister had not even thought it necessary to go to see her. It seems odd enough at first sight, that one, whose best loved place had ever been beside the bed of suffering, should have delayed so long, even if the invalid were not in danger, in visiting that of her own sister. But she was just at that time at the very height of the spiritual caresses by which God was repaying her life-long devotion to His service, and it seems probable or possible that while He was so pointedly soliciting her to divine love, she had some scruple or hesitation in yielding to that which was simply human in its nature. St. Albert, however, in answer to her prayers, commanded her to go at once, and she obeyed him. At the moment of her visit Elizabeth was, according to all human calculations, recovering, and her sister could detect no sign of death or of danger even, in her appearance. Moved nevertheless by an impulse for which she could not account, she left the invalid hastily, and going to the Carmelite Church, commenced a novena to St. Albert for her recovery. She was still upon her knees when the saint appeared to her, and told her that her sister's destiny was in her hands, and that she had but to say whether it should be life or death. He added, however, that Elizabeth was at that moment in the best possible disposition for dying well, whereas by a longer life her salvation would very probably be endangered. It was a sore trial, but Marie did not, could not hesitate after that. She loved her sister dearly, but her attachments were all of that higher order which seeks rather the real good of the beloved ones, than the purely selfish gratification to be derived from their personal presence, and she answered at once, that if such were the case, she could not oppose the designs of God upon her sister's soul, and that His will should be her will also. St Albert then bade her return to her sister's house, and prepare her for the last sacraments, adding that as soon as ever they had been administered, God would call her to Himself. Marie went at once, and found that even in the short interval of her own absence, a change for the worse had visibly taken place in the invalid. She admonished her gently of her situation, and sent for a priest, who, seeing her danger, administered at once all the rites of the Church to the dying woman; and at eight o'clock that very evening, Elizabeth had ceased to live! She appeared almost immediately afterwards to her sister, and told her that she was safe, but condemned for a time to the flames of purgatory. A few months afterwards, she reappeared bright and happy, and having given Marie to understand that the period of her purgation had been considerably shortened by her prayers and acts of self-denial, she told her that she needed them no longer. Elizabeth's husband remarried soon after her death, and rather than leave her sister's only remaining child to the proverbial mercies of a stepmother, Marie, who was already its godmother, and had had it christened by the name of Albertine, took it to her own home, and adopted it herself. She brought it up in a spirit of wisdom and unselfish tenderness rarely to be met with in such cases, adopted children being too often considered and treated as mere objects of amusement during the pretty helplessness of their babyhood, and of caprice, or of perhaps unkindness, when by their advance in age they have ceased to be interesting to their would-be benefactors. She taught Albertine her own occupation of needle-woman, grounding her at the same time with jealous care in the principles and practice of religion. Her own wishes for the child naturally pointed towards a convent, but finding as Albertine grew up that her vocation, like the mother's, was for the married state, she at once gave up her own ideas, and provided for her in the position to which God had called her, exactly as she would have done, if she had been a daughter of her own. Albertine became the mother of five children, and lived long enough to attend upon the death-bed of her aunt, dying herself, two years after Sœur Marie had gone to heaven, in such sentiments of piety and devotion as might reasonably have been expected from a person who had enjoyed, from her very cradle, the teaching as well as the example of a saint.

CHAPTER VII.

Freed by the death of her parents from many of the duties which had acted as a restraint upon her hitherto, Marie plunged more boldly than ever into that life of heroic charity, to which the spirit of God seems to have been urging her incessantly. She became as literally, the slave and servant of all who asked assistance at her hands, as if she had come into the world for no other purpose than to serve them, ready at a moment's notice to console the rich when they had need of consolation, to help the poor in their more material troubles, to visit the sick and those who were in prison, to aid the dying in the last awful struggle between grace and nature; and extending her charity beyond the grave, to pray and suffer afterwards for the departed soul, until the debts contracted during its earthly career were paid away, and cleansed from every stain of sin it took its flight at last to heaven.

For more than forty years, in fact, she may be

said with truth to have been at once the mother and the servant of all who were either poor, or sorrowful, or oppressed, in the great town of Liege. Her charity, moreover, was as enlightened as it was large. She was never (as good people too often are) superficial in her dealings with the poor. She visited them continually in their poor rooms and houses, heard from their own lips the story of their poverty, informed herself minutely as to their especial wants, and—which was the greatest charity of all—endeavored, even while relieving them for the moment, to place them in future above the necessity of asking alms, by procuring them work suitable, either to their capacity for labor, or to their original occupation. But until this latter object was accomplished, she never failed a day in bringing them food and fuel. If the latter were scarce, she used to make out of her ingenious charity, balls, (*hochets* the Liegois call them,) composed of cinders moistened and kneaded together with a little clay, which, when formed into balls and kindled, give a certain amount of heat; and if, as often enough happened, provisions were too dear for her scanty purse, she readily met the difficulty, by depriving herself of her mid-day meal, in order to

bestow it on the most destitute of her pensioners. She never told them, however, of her own privations, or allowed them to feel that they were in any way a burthen on her, and at the same time she was wisely careful in her endeavors to keep them up in those habits of self-respect which, out of the depths of their misery, the poor too often lose, helping and encouraging them for this purpose to cleanse their rooms and persons, and showing them how to mend their rags, so that their poverty might seem decent in the eyes of others. If they were shame-faced or depressed, she would try to cheer and reassure them by partaking with them of the food she brought, but as this of necessity diminished the little that she had to give, she much oftener left it entirely to them, and waited herself until evening in order to break her fast. Besides food and fuel, the money which Marie gave in charity seemed so much beyond what it was prudent or possible for a person living herself by the labor of her own hands to give, that her friends often shook their heads, and prophesied sad things as to the result of such uncalculating generosity. Among others, a religious, whom Marie held in great reverence for his many virtues, often tormented her by his reasons and remonstrances on the subject. Half in joke, but perhaps more than half in earnest, he used to accuse her, now of prodigality, now of imprudence, telling her that she ought to lay by something as a provision for her old age, and reminding her that she had also her little niece to educate and eventually to provide for,—winding up his arguments by a broad hint, that if she did not take his advice in time, she and her adopted child would be reduced at last to the ranks of that very poverty which she was now so zealous in relieving. To all this, and much more of the same kind, Marie had to listen often, but her answer was still the same:—"She had considered the matter well already—her friends, in fact, were not likely to allow her to forget it—nevertheless, she was still resolved to give so long as God gave her anything to give away; and as to her adopted child, she was God's child as well as hers, and so long as she served Him faithfully, she never doubted but that His Divine Providence would take care she needed nothing."

The good man would be silenced for the moment by this answer, but he never failed upon the first opportunity to return to the charge, asking her if she had at last begun to think of her old age, and if she had secured any sum of money in such a way that she could reckon upon it in the hour of need. "Yes," Marie once answered him, with a little smile of malicious triumph, "she had saved some money, and had put it out at interest, into hands where it was much safer than it could have been in her own." She meant, of course, that money given in charity was never lost, but was certain of making a good return upon some future day; and so her friend understood her. Nevertheless, he continued, time after time, to preach and remonstrate, until, weary of the contest, she complained tenderly to St. Francis Xavier, one of her favorite patrons, of the persecution she was undergoing, and of the efforts which were being made to withdraw her from the service of the poor.

It was almost immediately after receiving Holy Communion that she was moved to make this complaint, and in the midst of the hush and stillness which the sacred presence of her Lord yet made in her heart, she heard a voice which said distinctly, "Petite caissiere de Jesus Christ, donnez toujours."

The word "caissiere" was new to Marie, and as soon as ever she had finished her devotions, she went and asked its meaning of her director. When he had explained it to her, she was filled with consolation; and ever afterwards, while asking God to aid her in her efforts, she delighted in reminding Him that she did so only in the character which He himself had assigned to her, as the "petite caissiere" of His Divine Son.

Marie was not content with spending her own money on the poor. She zealously and generously accepted of that much harder part of charity, which consists in asking it of others. Many of the rich inhabitants of Liege responded nobly to these appeals, but others were less open-handed, and she had often enough occasions (occasions which she prized, perhaps, almost as much as she would have done success) of sharing in the opprobriums of her beloved poor, by being contemptuously refused. Whenever this happened, Marie made it a rule neither to answer or remonstrate, but retiring into the nearest Church, she would complain lovingly to Our Lord, not so much of those who had insulted and refused, as of Himself, and to Himself, the mover of all hearts, for permitting them to do so, asking Him with that simple *naiveté* which seems to have especially characterized the spirit of her prayer, if it was no longer His will that she should cater for the poor, and reminding him (as if she thought that he had forgotten) how impossible it would be for her to continue in her office as His "caissiere," if He did not or would not stir up the rich to help her.

It rarely happened that, after such a prayer as this, the aid she asked for was not accorded. Sometimes it came to her from friends, sometimes from mere acquaintances, or from strangers whom she had never even seen before, and upon more than one occasion, she found the money which she needed actually lying on the ground beside her, though she felt morally certain that it had not been there, when first she knelt down to pray. Whenever it came to her in this latter manner, it was always exactly the sum she needed, neither exceeding or falling short of it by a single farthing, a circumstance which confirmed her in her belief that it was a gift direct from the hands God Himself, and which justified her in her own eyes and in those of her director, in employing it for her intended purpose with as little scruple as if it had been put into her hand by an earthly acquaintance.

Once in possession of the coveted sum, she would fly with it to the objects of her pity, but, God so permitting it for her greater merit, it often happened that, when all glowing with joy she entered their houses, she was met with anger and complaints; the poor creatures, weary of the long delay, reproaching her with it as if it had been her fault, and sometimes even carrying their ingratitude so far as to insinuate, that she was keeping back a portion of the relief intended for them, for her own private use and benefit.

Such a check did not, and could not, destroy the joy of her soul in being able to give them aid, but it prevented it from flowing outwards, purifying it thus from all the dross of earthly feeling, and, by teaching her to look for her only recompense in the heart of her Divine Spouse, lifting her high above all thoughts of self, and enabling her to act wholly and solely for His dear sake, who has promised to regard each individual act of charity done towards the poor, as an act of charity performed especially to Himself. The way in which her kindness was received, never even tempted her to withdraw it. So far, indeed, was she from feeling angry, that albeit often wounded to the quick by these reproaches, they seem only to have added fuel to the fire of charity by which she was consumed, for she acknowledged to her director that she never felt more ready to toil and slave herself to death for the poor, than when by their murmurs and slanderous insinuations they were depriving her of all that natural human pleasure, which she would otherwise have felt in working for them.

No one who has studied the human heart, or who is conversant with the mental status of extreme poverty, will be much astonished at the fact that Sœur Marie was thus occasionally made the victim of their ingratitude. Misery often unveils weaknesses, which might never otherwise have been suspected there, in the heart of man, and if the rich seem free from some of the failings of the poor, it is simply because they have never been exposed to the same temptations. A due recognition of this fact would probably render us less harsh than we sometimes are in our language in their regard, for it seems to me that we often talk and think (some of us) a great deal more than is just or generous of their shortcomings on certain points, on which, having never felt any temptation to the contrary, we feel virtuously strong ourselves. Danger for the rich may lie in a direction, less perceptible to the human eye, but not less capable for that of effecting the shipwreck of the soul; and remembering this, let us ever be careful to speak tenderly, as well as to act generously, by the poor; contenting ourselves with the thought that in serving them we are serving their Lord and ours, whether we meet gratitude or ingratitude from them in return.

The abuse too often lavished upon Marie by her beloved poor, arose chiefly from a vulgar idea, that she would never have devoted her life as she had done to their service, if she had not in some way or other found profit in it for herself. There were minds among them too coarse to comprehend the Divine joys of charity to such a soul as Marie's, and too blunted by poverty to be able to comprehend the exquisite truth of our dear Lord's saying, that it is "a more blessed thing to give than to receive." A lesser measure of charity, a passing gift, an occasional service, they could have understood, but that any one should give all, and take nothing in return, seemed to them impossible; and therefore they were sometimes tempted to suspect that she appropriated to her own use a portion of the alms, which she had solicited and received in their name. Sometimes this suspicion moved them to such sentiments of anger, that they went further still in their accusations, daring to hint at dark and terrible things hidden beneath her garb of charity. One wretched woman, in particular, had the audacity to accuse her of the sin which was the most abhorrent of all to Marie's heart, seeing that it was in direct opposition to her own vow of chastity, and to the especial virtue of her blessed mother. Marie, in her innocent unconsciousness, did not at first comprehend the dark meaning of the insinuation, but a friend who chanced to be present at the moment, took the pains afterwards to enlighten her as to its nature, in order (I conclude) to induce her to discontinue her visits to the calumniator. It was the *one* point, the only one, upon which her soul could have been moved either to grief or anger. It offended alike, her feeling as a woman, as a religious, and a saint.

Nevertheless, she merely answered, with a smile, that, as the accusation was untrue, her friend need not trouble herself about it ; and that, for her own part, she would never allow the silly words of an angry woman to hinder her from a work of charity. Calmly, however, as she had spoken, she acknowledged afterwards to Pere Albert that she had felt the accusation bitterly, and that she had even to contend with a certain amount of repugnance (a very unusual thing with her) the next time she had occasion to visit her accuser. She went to her, notwithstanding, upon the very same day upon which she had been hitherto in the habit of seeing her, taking her revenge, after the fashion of the saints, by increasing her alms, and saying, in a half-joking, half-reproachful manner, as she gave it to her, "Here, my good friend, this money is your reward for having said such and such an evil thing of me on such and such a day."

For a moment the woman was shamed into contrition by this gentleness, and tried to excuse herself on the plea, that the greatness of her misery had filled her soul with bitterness, even towards her benefactors. It so happened that only two days afterwards she was sent to prison for some petty crime, a theft perhaps prompted by that very poverty which had led her to revile Marie, and the latter was no sooner made acquainted with the circumstance, than she set to work on her behalf, and never ceased exerting herself until she had succeeded in obtaining her discharge. It seems hard to believe in such ingratitude, but the wretched creature no sooner found herself at large, than she not merely renewed her previous calumny, but gave it point and meaning, by appealing to Marie's very efforts in her favor, as a proof that she feared discovery. This time she probably only said what she thought. Being utterly unequal to comprehend the heroic forgiveness of a saint, she came, as it were, almost inevitably to the conclusion, that Marie really had something to conceal, and that her kindness was, consequently, a mere bribe to silence. Another person, of the same intellectual calibre as this woman, carried her malice so far as to bring the slander in question to the notice of some ladies, who, having a high opinion of the sanctity of the sister, had always been liberal contributors to her various charities. Horrified at what they heard, and a little too ready, perhaps, to give credence to the tale, they sent at once for Marie, and overwhelmed her with reproaches. Her soul must have been stung to the quick as she listened to such words from women whom she both respected and loved, but she waited, as was her wont, until the first effervescence of their zeal had passed away, before attempting to say a syllable in her own defence. Then, in a few simple words, she explained to them how the slander had arisen, and left them not more astonished at her virtue, than touched and edified at the saintly meekness with which she had met the doubts they had been so carelessly cruel as to cast upon it. Notwithstanding these occasional ingratitudes, Marie loved her poor clients as if they had been her own children, the sick and infirm among them being ever the best tended and most cherished of the family. She served them in the hospitals, she sought them out in their lowest haunts, she journeyed from one end of the town to another on their behalf, Christ Himself urging and encouraging her in these charities, by sometimes leading her, in the visible form of a child, to houses where poor people, of whom she before knew nothing, were dying without aid or comfort for either soul or body. Once she had found them out, she set to work in earnest, making their beds, cleansing their rooms, relieving their persons of the dirt contracted by poverty and disease, dressing their wounds, fulfilling the lowest and most repulsive offices of charity in their regard, and even, like St. Francis Xavier, sucking their ulcers, whenever, like St. Francis Xavier, she felt any undue repugnance to the office. Nor did she limit her charity to procuring them the bare food and medicine needful for their recovery; over and above these things, Marie, like a tender mother, did her best to provide her patients with some of those lesser luxuries which sweeten life, and make illness itself endurable to the rich, but of which the poor, alas! have so seldom any portion.

When she had thus done all that she could for the welfare of their bodies, she went one step farther, and addressed her charity to their souls. She began by leading them to look gradually from herself, their visible benefactor, to Him, the invisible, by whose especial dispensation she had been sent to aid them; teaching them to feel, for the first time in their lives, perhaps, that they were objects of actual love and interest to that Almighty Father, in whose image they had been created. Love begets love, and having once convinced them that God really cared for them, she easily inspired them with the desire to love Him and serve Him in return. This fact established, the rest of her task was comparatively easy. To love Him, they must know Him, and to know Him they must listen to the teachings of religion. Marie dealt with them afterwards according to the measure of their previous knowledge. Such of them as were absolutely ignorant, she instructed in the catechism, others who had been merely neglectful of their duties, she advised and exhorted, as the Holy Spirit moved her, to confession, preaching not less powerfully by words than by example, and by this twofold medium, bringing numbers to the sacraments who had absented themselves for years, and ensuring a happy death to hundreds of others, who, but for her interference, would have departed this world unaided by the saving graces of Extreme Unction, or by even the presence of a priest.

Besides her ordinary routine of work, Marie was seldom unprovided with some extraordinary and accidental case of suffering whereon to exercise her zeal. Among the men employed in the collieries of Liege, she found especially frequent occupation. These poor creatures, like all others called to underground pursuits, were too frequently in a state of the grossest ignorance. Dwellers, from their childhood upwards, of the mines, and only returning to the surface of the earth when night and weariness were calling imperatively for repose, they were so entirely cut off from every ordinary practice of religion, that it was much if they had not forgotten even the very articles of faith which are needful for salvation. Being subject from the nature of their occupations to serious accidents; and poverty, and the maladies which poverty almost always brings in its train, being besides frequent visitors in their households, they were oftener than almost any other class of the Liegois population compelled to have recourse to the charity of Marie. Whenever this happened, she, knowing their little means of acquiring knowledge in the science of religion, exerted herself to the utmost to induce them to accept of a regular course of catechetical instruction, and as their previous neglect had proceeded more from ignorance than vice, she had generally the happiness of succeeding in her efforts, and of seeing them return, good practical Catholics, to their dangerous occupations. Plague, a far more common visitor in those days than it is in ours, among the crowded cities of the west, gave her occasions for the exercise of heroic charity, which she seized upon with avidity. Two or three times at least, while she lived, it spread desolation through her native town, and wherever it raged most fiercely, there she was invariably to be found, braving death in its most terrible aspect for the relief of the sufferers. It was generally brought to the city by foreign ships; the authorities of Liege, therefore, established a law of quarantine, by which passengers were compelled to remain on board for a given number of days after the arrival of their vessel in the river. This quarantine was no doubt necessary for the health of the inhabitants, but it was a terrible hardship, and often, even a direct cause of disease and death, to those subjected to its regulations. As an instance of this, we are told that, upon one occasion a troopship, closely packed with soldiers, came up the river for the purpose of landing her passengers at Liege. It having been ascertained, however, by the magistrates of the city that a case of plague had already occurred on board, permission to do so was refused them, and they were compelled to endure all the miseries of protracted quarantine in a crowded, unhealthy vessel. The consequences may easily be imagined. Sick and well cooped up together, the disease spread like wild-fire; fever and dysentery followed plague; and from the month of October to the ensuing May, such of these poor wretches as had survived the trial, led what may be styled a living death among their dead and dying comrades. During the whole of that time Marie devoted herself almost entirely to their service. By dint of begging all over the town, she procured them medicines, clothing, and fresh food, everything, in fine, calculated to check disease or cure it. Not content with this, she took upon herself the charge of nursing, and spent night and day beside the sick in order to make sure that none departed this life unfortified by the sacraments, either going herself or sending for a priest, the moment she detected signs of danger. The Jesuits were her zealous co-operators in this work of love, and two of them having caught the disease, died martyrs to their charity. Marie was filled with a holy envy of their happiness, and could hardly console herself because God had not thought her worthy of a similar favor. That, however, which she longed for, her director, knowing how useful her life was among the poor of Liege, dreaded continually on her account. He could not, indeed, forbid her to console by her presence this poor plague-stricken company, but he remonstrated with her often on the closeness of her attendance, and on the danger which she incurred of falling a victim to the malady. Probably Marie knew better than he did the designs of God in the matter, for she used only to answer with a little smile and a sigh, that he might make himself perfectly easy on her account, the honor and joy of such a martyrdom not being reserved for her.

Once Marie had undertaken the charge of a sick person, she never failed or faltered in her attendance, however tedious the malady might prove to be, redoubling her attentions as the hour of death drew near From the moment in fact, when the symptoms had become unmistakable, she never left her patients, either consoling and encouraging, or exciting them, as the nature of the case demanded, to repentance, but ever observing such sweet measure in her exhortations as that sorrow for sin should never weaken hope, or hope strengthen itself into such forgetfulness of past error as might border on presumption. She was careful, moreover, not to weary or disgust them by long exercises of devotion, but kneeling quietly beside them, she prayed for them for hours in the interior of her own soul, sprinkling them occasionally with holy water, or giving them the cross to kiss, and rousing their attention every now and then by short ejaculatory prayers, pronounced aloud with a fervor and unction which communicated itself at once not only to the heart of the dying person, but also to the hearts of all who heard her.

Marie did not limit these offices of charity to such persons only, as she had waited on in sickness. Unthought of and unasked for, she was nevertheless often a welcome and most useful visitor beside the death-bed of patients who had either never known her, or who had thought but little of her, in their days of health and vigor. Friend or foe, or absolutely unknown, it was enough for her to be made aware that a human brother was going to his last account, to rouse up all her zeal and charity, and to compel her, as it were, to interfere in his behalf. The bell which tolls the agony,—the passing bell, as we call it still in England, (where we have retained the name and memory of the thing, without, alas! its real meaning,)—had scarcely announced, by the sad irregular beatings of its great heart, that a soul just entering into its agony was thus touchingly appealing to its living brothers for prayers in its last hour of trial, ere Marie was in the presence of the dying person. No matter what her occupation at the time might be,—from her work, from her prayers, from her very bed she arose up at once, and went on her way with such swiftness and impetuosity, and so sure an instinct as to the exact quarter of the town in which her services were required, that people could not but confess that it must have been a spirit all on fire with the love of God and a holy hunger for the salvation of souls, which impelled her footsteps.

Many a poor soul owed, to all human appearance, its salvation to these impromptu visits. Sometimes she could guess from the merely external circumstances of the case, that the dying person was not in a fit state to meet his God; but just as often she was made aware of this fact by what appears to have been an especial inspiration of the Holy Ghost. In either case, she never rested until the invalid had been brought to better sentiments, and a priest had been sent for, for the administration of the sacraments.

Once—it was her cousin who told the story to Pere Albert—she heard the passing bell tolling from the church of St. Aldegonde, which stood at quite the opposite end of the town from the "Place des Jesuites," (I know not if it be called so still,) where she herself resided. She set out at once, going with such rapidity, that it almost seemed, even to herself, as if she were being transported thither by the invisible medium of the angels, and she scarcely knew where she was, ere she found herself close to the house of the dying person.

Entering it without ceremony, she passed at once,

as was her custom, into the sick-chamber. It was filled with friends of the dying man, who were crowding round his bed with much anxiety for his bodily condition, but with little heed or care, it appeared to Marie, for the yet more terrible maladies of his soul. Kneeling down beside him, she prayed for a long time fervently and in silence for him, then rising up, she spoke to him and tried to persuade him to join her in such ejaculatory prayers as seemed best suited to his state of weakness. She soon discovered, by his answers to her exhortations, that he was dying without the sacraments. No one, in fact, of all those who were lamenting so loudly, had even thought of sending for a priest; and he himself was far too near extremity to be capable of expressing, or perhaps of feeling even, any wish or anxiety upon the subject. Marie instantly supplied the omission. She sent for a priest, and after waiting until he had arrived, and until all the sacraments of the church had been administered, she waited yet a little longer, until death had claimed his victim. The intervening moments were employed by her in consoling and encouraging the poor dying creature, and she succeeded at last in infusing such love and fervor into his soul by her words of fire, that, contrary to all expectation, he breathed his last in sentiments of charity and contrition which gave every hope and almost certainty, to his friends, of the salvation of his soul.

Marie had something of the spirit of the good old Tobias in her character. She had an especial reverence for the dead, and whenever any of her clients were poor and friendless, she, poor as she was herself, never hesitated to take into her own hands the charges of their funeral, and of the prayers and masses which were afterwards to be said for their souls. This being well known in Liege, whenever any of its poorer population met with a sudden or violent death, the cares and expenses of their funeral were almost certain to devolve on her. For there existed in those days a law in Liege, by which it was forbidden to any one, in case of violent death, to remove, or even to touch the corpse, until persons deputed for the purpose (*gens de justice*, as they were called) had examined the body, and pronounced upon the cause, as well as upon the fact itself, of death. All this requiring a certain amount of time and trouble, people soon learned to cut the matter short by sending for Marie, who gladly undertook the task of communicating with the authorities, after which, if the deceased was poor, or a stranger in the city, she buried him at her own expense. Nor did her charity end at the death-bed or in the grave of those in whose favor it had once been enlisted. It followed them beyond the tomb! She thought of them continually in that fiery purgation into which, too probably, the tenor of their past lives had cast them, and she prayed and mortified herself severely on their account, in order that they might all the sooner be cleansed from sin, and in a fit state to behold their God. How pleasing this devotion was to that heavenly Father, whose justice compels Him to punish even while He is yearning for the embraces of His guilty but repentant children, He himself was pleased to show, by allowing her frequent and joyous visitations from the souls of those, whose sufferings she had lightened or shortened by her prayers. They generally came to her, in the first instance, soon after death, to declare the state in which they found themselves, and after humbly acknowledging the faults for which they were in durance, to ask her to aid them by prayers and pilgrimages, and other sufferings, severer still to human nature, and more analogous to the nature of the sins for which they had been condemned. But they seldom failed to visit her at last, radiant in gladness and in glory, to thank her for all that she had done for them, and to promise her in return their prayers and abundant supplications in the heaven to which, by her charity, she had hastened their arrival. And it was not only the souls of those whom in lifetime she had befriended who thus appealed to her! Many whom she had never before known, or even heard of, were permitted to visit her in a similar manner, and to ask her for aid in their fiery trial. But as these visitations will form a portion of an ensuing chapter in the life of the Sister, I will merely pause here to remark that she revealed them to no one but to Pere Albert, to whom as her director, she was compelled to go for guidance, and that even to him she never mentioned the names of the persons demanding succor, for she held herself bound, and very properly, to secrecy in such matters, as much as if they had been actually communicated to her under the seal of auricular confession.

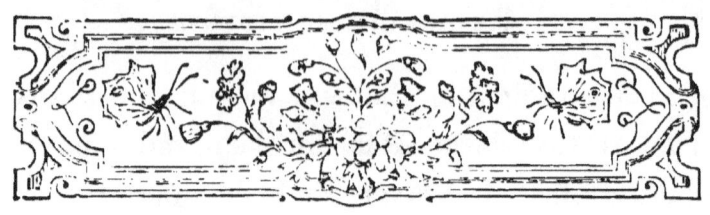

CHAPTER VIII.

Among the many other charitable institutions with which Liege in those days abounded, it possessed one, the most useful and heroic perhaps of any, for the aid and instruction of poor prisoners,—those alike who were condemned to captivity for debt, or who were enduring it as the expiation of their crimes. Ever foremost where the welfare of her neighbor was concerned, Marie eagerly enrolled herself as a member of this confraternity, and as might easily have been expected from her antecedents, she soon became one of the most zealous and efficient of its members. The poor prisoners themselves loved her and called her mother, and a veritable mother, in fact, she ever was to them, caring for, and doing for them such services as a mother by the laws of nature would have done only for her own child. Her tact in their regard was only equalled by her zeal, and both had been so well proved by the authorities, that the prison gates were open to her by day or night, whenever she chose to enter them,—the chiefs of the confraternity, and the very jailers themselves, being in the invariable habit of sending for her, whenever any extraordinary case of crime or misfortune seemed to require extraordinary delicacy of treatment. She never entered the prison without bringing with her some little alms or luxury, if not for all, at any rate for the most needy, for she had thoroughly realised the fact that such people are generally little more than grown-up children, whose hearts must be won in the first instance by some material kindness, if afterwards they are to be spiritualized and directed towards God. When she had fed them and clothed them, and thus made them comprehend how entirely she had their best interests at heart, she began to speak to them of their captivity and to console them—not foolishly—lamenting over their misery, and charging their judges and accusers with injustice, but with wise and gentle firmness, making them thoroughly comprehend that their chains were the just punishment and inevitable end of crime, and yet soothing them at the same time by tenderly suggesting that it depended only upon themselves, and upon the spirit in which they endured their punishment, to make it a matter of merit as well as of necessity. She often told them with a noble hardihood, which seldom failed of making an impression, that many were saved in prison, and by the restraints of prison, who out of it would have lost their souls, and she added, that if it were only for this very reason, that by the impossibility of quitting it, they were prevented from offending God by mortal sin, they ought to kiss its very walls in gratitude for the refuge thus afforded them against themselves. When they were sad and desponding, she cheered them by her gentle gaiety; when they were inclined to grumble, she tried to induce them to dwell less upon the severity of man, by whom their punishment had been decreed, than upon the goodness of God, who had permitted it to be carried into effect, solely in order that, while the body was weighed down by chains, the soul might have liberty to soar towards Him, and so draw down upon itself such abundant showers of Divine grace as might ultimately secure for it salvation. And all this was said with such a tender, loving grace, not laid down in set or wearisome discourses, but suggested rather by a word dropped here and there, as if by accident, whenever the occasion offered, that men who would have been deaf to the eloquence of a Massillon, and who had remained obstinately cold to the teaching of the reverend Father of the prison, became docile as little children in the hands of Sœur Marie. The Sister made no distinction in her kindness between those who were in prison for debt and those who were condemned to it for crime, save only, that considering the spiritual needs of the latter to be the greatest, she surpassed herself (if that were possible) in tenderness in their regard. Prisoners for debt she aided chiefly by begging for them from door to door until she had amassed a sum sufficient to set them at liberty, or she called upon the creditors, and never left them peace or rest until they had consented either to forgive a portion of the debt, or to remit it altogether. But to those who were in captivity for crime she gave a yet more minute and personal attention, spending hours upon their instruction, and going over and over again with them, with a patience which never failed or faltered, one by one, all those articles of faith, of which, however needful to salvation, they were either unhappily in ignorance altogether, or had totally forgotten since the days when they heard them in childhood. While engaged in this occupation she often spent entire nights and days in prison with her catechists; soothing, and at the same time instructing, charming away the horrors of that abode of gloom by teaching them tne sweet music of the name of Jesus, and yet urging them all the while without remission to the sterner lesson of searching their souls and consciences for the sins which had brought them hither. In order fully to appreciate the merit of this voluntary sojourn among its inhabitants, it is needful to remember that prisons in the days of Sœur Marie were conducted in a very different spirit from what they are at present. It was towards the close of an iron age—men thought little of comfort in their own homes, still less in the abodes which were consecrated to the punishment of crime! Prisons, whether they were the cachettes of the feudal castle, or places of detention erected within the walls of a fortified city, were built for the most part in such a manner that the cells of the criminals were under ground, deprived, in a great measure, of light and air, and as a necessary consequence, the natural abodes of plague and fever.

Filth, which it was no one's business to remove, lay everywhere in heaps; fog-damps filled the cells, and their walls were stained and mottled with moss and lichens growing abundantly in that unwholesome moisture; rats ran unmolested over the bodies of the prisoners and robbed them of their very food; insects and disgusting reptiles crawled upon the slimy floors; and every stalk and fibre of the straw, which, once laid down for bedding, was never changed until its occupant had left the prison for liberty or death, was a living nest of vermin. Neither scourge or hair-shirts, therefore, could have afforded to a delicately-minded woman such an entire measure of mortification as was contained in the mere fact of an hour spent in such an abode; and Marie spent, as we have seen, not one hour only, but often the twenty-four, without rest or remission, in the midst of these abominations. Her chief anxiety and most unremitting love were of course reserved for those poor wretches whose sentence was the scaffold. She was sent for the moment a fatal judgment had been pronounced, so that, " More work now for Marie Sellier," became a sort of proverb in the town upon such occasions. In cases such as these Marie had a mode of management especially her own. Pondering often upon those words of her Divine Spouse, "that there were certain devils which could only be exercised by prayer and fasting," she had arrived at last at the conclusion, that to cast out the demons, already in possession of it, from a human soul, maddened by their suggestions and by the sentence impending over it to despair, was a task even more difficult, if indeed it were not actually the same work under another aspect, as that of expelling them from the body. She began the work, therefore, by making of her whole person a living sacrifice on their behalf. For them she put up her most fervent prayers, making them for the time being almost the sole object of her communications, with her heavenly Spouse; for them she fasted night and day; for them she tore her innocent body with disciplines of chains, and clothed it from head to foot with hair-cloth; and after she had thus done all that was possible for them, short of injury to life, by the chastisement of her own person, she sought out every priest she knew, begging his masses for the same intention, and recommending it besides to the devout prayers of every religious body with which she happened to be acquainted. Never until she had thus, as she hoped, enlisted Heaven itself in the cause of his conversion, did Marie venture to enter into the presence of the condemned; and then her success was almost always certain, being commensurated with the pains which she had taken to secure it.

The fathers who had charge of the prisoners used, in fact, to say that she did the most difficult part of their work for them, by smoothing their way and leading the mind of the poor sinner almost insensibly back to such a sentiment and knowledge of religion, as enabled them to set the seal upon his conversion by the speedy administration of the sacraments. She evidently possessed a knowledge of the human heart, and a tact in addressing herself to its better feelings, which was no doubt the result at once and reward of the prayers and mortification by which she had inaugurated the good work; for she seems to have had no precise or settled method of proceeding—her way being different with each individual mind with which she was brought in contact, so that almost unconsciously to herself she suited the very inflexions of her voice, as well as the whole tenor of her instructions, to the special requirements of the case before her. If she found the condemned exasperated against his judges, she placed before his mind's eye the innocence of Jesus, and urged upon him the beautiful necessity thus laid upon his soul, of pardoning, even as his Divine Lord had done before him, both his judges and accusers. When there could be little doubt as to the essential justice of the sentence, she had, moreover, sufficient moral courage to take the part of those who had pronounced it, maintaining that they had only done their duty, and reminding her penitent at the same time of the good thief, who, far from denying or excusing, had openly and humbly acknowledged his own guilt, and thus won for himself that sweet response of Jesus: "Amen, I say to thee, this day shalt thou be with Me in Paradise."

If the condemned affected to bravado and to make light of his coming doom, she told him with an air of cold indifference, which had even more effect than the words themselves, that she set but little value on a firmness which, arising as often from vanity or from natural constitution as from any higher motive, was even more a heathen than a Christian virtue. The courage which spurns at death, she said, must spring from a higher source than mere carelessness of life or indifference to pain—it must proceed either from a loving desire to see God, or from sorrow for the sin by which He has been offended, or from a generous contempt for that life which has been the means whereby the offence has been committed; and thus, little by little, she tried to make him feel that if only for this very reason, it would be better far, to desire with the apostle, to be "dissolved and to be with Christ."

If, on the contrary, she found him cast down by sadness or tempted to despair, she reminded him that after all he was only called upon to endure, a little sooner than perhaps nature had intended, that which each individual member of the family of Adam would, in the end, be compelled to undergo. The manner of death might indeed be different, but the fact was the same for all, as difficult and as bitter for the old as for the young, as difficult and as bitter, or even more so, on a bed of down as on the gallows—the only real softener of its pangs being the spirit in which it was accepted. All men therefore might be considered as criminals under sentence of death, for Christ alone died wholly innocent, and if He chose to die by the hand of the executioner, it was chiefly in order that none might be able, or have the temptation to say, that their chalice was more bitter than His. By his death upon Mount Calvary, He had sanctified the very gallows; and those consequently who were condemned to it, had but to unite themselves to Him in spirit in order to share in all His merits, had but to say, as He had said already in the Garden, "Fiat voluntas tua," in order afterwards to be able to add, with a good hope of its being accepted, His last touching address to that Heavenly Father, who, thanks be to His loving condescension, is now our father as well as His: "Father, into Thy hands I commend My spirit."

I have recorded these instructions because they seem to me so full of wisdom, not to be acquired in any mere school of human learning, that they tell more of the deep sanctity of Marie's hidden life than whole pages devoted to describing it in any other way could possibly have done. Her director was of the same opinion, for though he felt a great dislike to the sort of *eclat* which this office of consoler to the condemned shed round Marie; and though he considered it as one by no means desirable or suitable to a woman, he nevertheless could not resolve to forbid her its acceptance, convinced as he was by long experience that God Himself was her inspiration, and that the salvation of a human soul would prove almost inevitably its result. It was partly perhaps in deference to this opinion, but chiefly, probably, from her natural repugnance, as a woman, to such scenes, that Marie never accompanied her charge to the scaffold itself, albeit there more than ever he might have seemed in need of her gentle whisper of encouragement. During that awful half hour of suspense, she remained in the prison praying fervently until all was over, a fact which she often knew before it was officially announced, by the reappearance of the victim, permitted by God to visit her even on the instant of his death, in order to thank her in the first place for her good offices in the past, and to entreat her in the next, to continue them a little longer for his deliverance from purgatory. Such a communication was always a signal to her to commence a fresh series of fasts and penances, so that each of the poor souls whom she had thus fitted for death may be said to have cost her a double tide of suffering: the first, in order to save them from the pangs of hell; the second, to obtain from them a speedier participation in the joys of Heaven.

Upon only one occasion is it recorded that she accompanied her penitent to the actual place of execution. The object of this extra act of charity was a poor wretch who would, it seemed likely, prove contumacious to the last, he having during the whole term of his residence in prison refused positively to forgive certain persons against whom he had a grudge. They had probably been in some way or other accessory to his condemnation, and his soul was in consequence filled with bitterness against them. Priests and religious had exhorted and reasoned with him in vain, and at last, in despair, they gave him over to Marie. Her success, however, for once, was no greater than their own. She left no means untried to move him, visiting him both night and day, waiting and watching for a mental change, but that change never came! Anything else she might easily have persuaded him to do, but to forgive his enemies he would not; and knowing that if God is merciful He is also just, and that by the measure which we measure out to others, He too will meet out to ourselves, Marie began in the end to despair of his salvation. The day and hour arrived at last, and he was still in the same mood when the officers of justice came to fetch him. Marie could not make up her mind to abandon him in that dreadful state, and hoping still against hope, that even at the last moment he might surrender himself to the teachings of religion, she followed him to the place of execution, and from the window of a friend's house, just opposite the scaffold, watched and prayed during the tragedy which followed.

She knew indeed intuitively that nothing could convert him *then*, and yet she put up her petitions as earnestly as if she still retained some hope upon the subject; for she was given to see, as in a vision, how the grace of God was ready to fall upon his soul in showers if only he would have deigned, not so much even to ask for it, as to accept of it unasked, and how his ultimate perdition would be accomplished by hardening himself against the interior inspirations thus sent him from above, just as he had previously hardened himself against the counsels and exhortations of the holy men who had attended him in prison.

The smallest of those inspirations, if he would but have adopted it, might have saved him; but one after another he rejected them, and at each new rejection she beheld the devils, who were already clinging round their victim, pressing closer and closer still, feeding his heart with fresh thoughts of rage, and urging his mind to newer and more hideous blasphemies against God than any of which he had been even capable before. Sad and sorrowful his angel guardian still lingered at his side upon the scaffold, in heaven Mary and the saints still solicited his pardon, and God Himself still looked down pitifully upon him, ready, at the first symptoms of softening on his part, to pardon all; so that his final condemnation became less a sentence enforced against him, than one which he himself had deliberately pronounced upon his own soul. Thus he remained even to the end, hardened and unrepenting, and at the very instant when his head fell upon the scaffold, Marie beheld his soul carried away in triumph by the devils, who had so successfully contended with God and man for its possession. The dismal sight filled her with such agony of soul and body that she nearly fainted; and for many days afterwards she suffered from serious illness, caused by the bare recollection of the misery which he had thus invoked upon himself.

Prisoners, though very dear to her soul, were not, however, the only public sinners who were the objects of Marie's pious efforts. Zeal for souls devoured her; and it soon became evident to her director that she was one of those innocent and devoted beings whom God had chosen, as it is every now and then His custom, to interpose between sinners and His justice. The thought of their damnation was night and day before her eyes, and she offered herself up continually, to suffer in body and soul all and everything that a human creature is capable of enduring, so only that their souls might be saved alive. God no doubt inspired these desires; and he at once accepted and rewarded them by a fresh access of suffering, every time the wilful wickedness of some particular soul whom He desired to save made a fresh demand upon His justice, for as Marie herself once said, with the simple *naivete* which formed the groundwork of her character, "When a soul once asks for sufferings for the sake of sinners, God does not make it wait long for the response." It would take pages to tell what she endured in her own person by her voluntary mortifications, or what God gave her, over and above, to suffer, in order to fill up the measure of His justice, by sickness, by mental anguish, by the persecution of men, and by the attacks of the demons whom for long years of her life He permitted bodily to torment her.

And the reward of this martyrdom of love found itself, as we have already seen, in a power over the minds of sinners, which, once exercised, they were rarely capable of resisting; a tact which never failed; and an intuitive knowledge of the interior state of the person whom she addressed, which enabled her at once to tax him openly with his crime, and so either to shame or induce him to amendment.

Being one day in ecstacy, her cousin, knowing that in such a state she was compelled to answer to many things upon which at other times humility made her silent, took the opportunity of asking her how it happened that she managed to deal successfully with certain sinners, seeing that of the precise nature of their sin she had been all her life-time preserved, by the grace of God, absolutely ignorant. It is true, Marie answered instantly. "It is true that of that particular sin I know as little as a child of two years old, nevertheless when my Divine Spouse wills me to withdraw any one from its commission, He Himself teaches me what to say, so that for the time being, I understand and discourse upon it, as well as if I were a theologian."

And that this was but the simple truth seemed evident from the whole tenor of her life and conduct. The bare mention of this vice filled her with such horror upon ordinary occasions that she retired the moment it became, even indirectly, the subject of conversation; and yet if a soul were to be saved from its commission, she spoke up at once and so effectually that she rarely failed in her object.

Happening one day to enter a church she saw a young girl, something in whose look and manner, as she spoke to another person, led her to suspect of bad intentions. Marie knew nothing of her antecedents, having never even seen her before; but, zeal for God's glory urging her to interfere, she waited until her companion had retired, and then without ceremony accosted her. The girl was only too glad of a confidant. She was not vicious but very poor, and poverty was rapidly urging her to ruin when Marie thus interposed to save her. She willingly consented to follow the sister to her humble home; and there Marie kept her until evening, taking advantage of the visit to represent to her in all its horrors the life she had been tempted to commence—the offence to God—the scandal to the good—the misery so certain in the end to follow—the loss of honor—and finally damnation. The poor girl wept as she listened, and readily promised to renounce her evil projects; Marie undertaking on her part to procure her sufficient work to enable her to live respectably in future by the labor of her own hands.

The devil had counted securely on his victim, and he was furious in proportion at her conversion. He showed his finger openly, in fact, for while

Marie was cutting out some work to give her, he struck the scissors out of her hand, declaring that if she did not desist in this work of charity, he would set the whole on fire. Marie however was by this time used to his attacks, and had learned like St. Teresa to care no more for his ravings than for the buzzings of a fly: she therefore told him quietly that he had better depart and leave her in peace, for that if he did not, she would double the good work by giving to her convert the whole of the piece of stuff which she had in her hand, instead of only a portion, as she had intended at first. Another girl she once met as she was going to mass, and it was given to her internally to comprehend that the soul of this young person was in sin. Scarcely had she received the intimation ere the girl of her own accord accosted her, recommending herself to her prayers and acknowledging at the same time that four entire years had passed since she had been permitted to receive Communion. She had never indeed absolutely left off confession, but the priest she said to whom she had been in the habit of addressing herself, had been so severe with her on her sinful inclinations, that she had finally cast off all restraint, and had begun, not only to lead a bad life boldly in her own person, but had induced many of her young companions to follow her example. Now at last, however, the grace of God had so effectually touched her heart, that she was quite resolved to go to confession in good earnest, if only that Marie would promise in the meantime to pray for her herself, and to get a Mass said besides for her entire conversion. Marie with all her gentleness, could be severe enough when there was occasion for it; and moreover, she never could endure to hear any one unjustly blamed. Without any circumlocution, therefore, she told the girl that the priest had acted properly in her regard, for that so long as she chose to persist in a life of sin, so long he would never have been justified before God in throwing pearls to swine by permitting her to approach Communion. Since, however, she had now at last resolved upon conversion, Marie told her she had no longer any cause for despondency; she had but to put her confidence in God and Our Blessed Lady, and go boldly to confession. The priest would soon discover that there was no longer a sufficient reason for refusing her Communion, and in order to aid her in the great work which she had in hand, Marie promised, moreover, to have a Mass said for her immediately before the altar of

St. Remi. The girl left her promising to obey her to the letter, but she was no sooner out of sight than Marie discovered, to her infinite annoyance, that she had not so much as a single sou about her, wherewith to procure the Mass. In her childlike confidence she had instantly recourse to Mary, and scarcely was her prayer concluded ere she discovered something which, on nearer inspection, proved to be a piece of money, just sufficient, and no more, to enable her to fulfil her promise, glittering on the ground beside her. She took it at once to church, and the poor girl having by this time finished her confession, was enabled to communicate at the very Mass thus mercifully provided for her. This conversion proved solid and enduring, and the girl thus rescued from the grasp of Satan, often returned to Marie to receive her counsels, and to thank her for the wise mixture of tenderness and severity by which alone she acknowledged it could have been perfectly accomplished.

In this way, or in others, somewhat similar, Marie became the confidant and spiritual adviser of hundreds, who were moved, as it seemed, by an especial inspiration of the Holy Ghost to confide their misery to her. Some among these poor creatures had been tempted to despair by want, some by the loss of friends, or other temporal misfortunes,—many by the consciousness of secret sin,—and not a few of the latter had even so far yielded to despondency as to have attempted suicide, and were actually bleeding from injuries inflicted on their own persons, when they were forced, as it were, in their own despite, to seek out Marie and deposit their sorrows in her bosom. These she frequently healed, body and soul, by the mere touch of her fingers, as she dressed their gaping wounds; others she consoled with gentle words; and from others she contrived to remove temptations: so that as a matter of fact, it might be truly said that no one ever left her presence without having received the double blessing of a reconciliation with God and with themselves. Upon other occasions, instead of sinners coming to her, Marie herself was compelled to seek them out, by an impulse which she could neither account for nor resist, and this frequently, without any previous knowledge whatever of the persons to whose assistance she had been sent. Led thus by the Spirit of God, she would enter houses where she had never been before, or which she had visited only for the purpose of giving alms, and the doors seeming to open to her of their own accord, she would find herself face to face with persons bent evidently upon committing sin. Whether she was acquainted with them or whether she was not, was all the same to her! She saw only the offence to God and the injury to souls which was sure to follow; and filled with grief and holy indignation, addressed them in terms which nothing less than the Spirit of God could have given her courage to employ, or them, perhaps, patience to endure. Mute and shame-faced they stood before her, while she reproached them with their evil thoughts and dealings, until unable to excuse themselves by a single word, they shrank off to their several homes. "Folly and imprudence!" the world might be tempted to cry out, but that hers was the true folly of the cross, and an imprudence prompted and authorized by her Divine Spouse Himself is proved by the fact, that upon no such occasion did any one ever attempt to insult her or do her harm. The love of God was so evidently the source of all she said and did, and her face and voice grew so eloquent as she pleaded for Him with His creatures, that even if these latter were not persuaded to amend, they felt no desire to avenge themselves on His faithful and zealous little handmaid.

She was sometimes sent, however, in a yet more marked and particular manner to the aid of a faltering spirit. The town of Liege was very strict in the enforcement of the moral law, and persons who had become liable to punishment on account of its infraction, used often to fly to Maestricht, a town in Holland, in which greater liberty was permitted, and which became, in consequence, a very den of iniquity and a refuge for all the vicious and dissolute of the surrounding country.

Did a poor girl fall into sin, and fear to return to her parents' house, her first thought was Maestricht, and hither she at once turned her footsteps, knowing well that, amid the dissolute crowds which filled its streets, persons far guiltier than herself might easily pass muster. Once within its gates she soon lost all idea of fear or shame, so that to say a girl had fled to Maestricht was much the same thing as to assert that she was half-way to hell already.

To this city of lost souls Marie was naturally often compelled to go in pursuance of her sublime vocation. Sometimes she went to seek out persons to whom she was already known, and in whom therefore she was naturally interested, but just as often it was in pursuit of sinners with whose fall and flight she could only have become acquainted by the direct interposition of her Divine Spouse Himself.

Thus, one night in the month of January soon after she had lain down to rest, it was intimated to her that a young girl, of whom she had no previous knowledge of any kind, poor, and desperate in her poverty, had just left the town in order to add one to the many who led the life of the reprobate at Maestricht.

Marie was wearied out by a long day's work, and she had, moreover, been previously tormented the night before by demons, from whose ill treatment she was still enduring agonies, but it was enough for her to know that a soul for which Christ had died was in danger of its salvation in order to induce her to start at once upon her doubtful mission. The night was cold, and dark, and dreary. There was a bitter frost upon the ground; and when, tired and shivering, she at last reached the city gates, she found that the person of whom she was in search had passed through them at an earlier hour, and was, therefore, in all probability, already a long way upon her road. Marie would not, for all that, give up the chase, and by dint of hard running, she overtook her at last at about a league from Liege. She accosted her at once, remonstrating, promising, and persuading; and in the end, after a hard battle between the grace of God and the promptings of the devil, she succeeded in inducing her to give up her evil project, and to return to a respectable life at Liege.

This time the zealous little sister escaped without personal injury to herself, but she was not always so fortunate, for the devil and his emissaries often met her on her return from similar expeditions and dragged her violently along the ground, declaring with horrible imprecations, that as she had robbed them of their lawful prey, they would sooner or later take possession of her own body and soul instead. But Marie met them, as ever was her wont, with a smile of scorn, and, having put them to flight by the sign of the cross, she re-entered her humble home, glad and triumphant in the thought, that another soul had been added by her means to the list of those for whom the precious blood of Jesus Christ has not been shed in vain.

CHAPTER IX.

We have seen in the preceding chapter that God, in the inscrutable mystery of His dealings with His creatures, had given permission to the demons to torment His faithful little handmaid; that permission being, however, evidently accompanied by the same restriction which He laid upon them in the case of His servant Job,—namely, that they should not touch her life. Like St. Anthony, like St. Teresa, like the saintly Curé d'Ars, she was subject night or day to these terrible visitations, and, like the latter also, the worst and most painful of the number, were almost invariably either followed or preceded by the conversion of some great sinner. They appeared to her visibly in all sorts of shapes and varieties of figure, sometimes like wild beasts; at others, in their own more terrible identity, as demons, roaring, threatening, and blaspheming, in order to terrify and confound her; or more dangerously and insidiously still, Lucifer endeavored in the guise of some saint, most usually of her especial patron St. Albert, to ingratiate himself into her confidence, and to detach her by counsels, apparently wise and emanating from true anxiety for her salvation, from that confidence and obedience to her director, which he knew full well to be the best assurance for success in the battle of life—needed by every Christian soul, but, for one destined as Marie evidently was, to walk in those higher paths of the spiritual life where a fall is almost certain to be fatal—absolutely indispensable. Failing, as of course he always did fail in these attempts, he had recourse to rougher methods, and Marie was often seized upon, dragged backwards and forwards along the ground, and struck and beaten as mercilessly as if she had been a dog.

If it happened to be in the winter season, the demons tore her out of her bed and plunged her over and over again in the waters of a deep well which chanced to be in the court outside, hardly allowing her time to breathe as she came to the surface, ere they pushed her down again. When they left her at last, she lay from exhaustion more dead than alive upon the pavement, and, by the time that she had found strength to return to her own room, her dress had become so stiff and congealed by the freezing of the water with which it was saturated, that she was often compelled to tear and cut it, by main force, from off her person. Sometimes she was even unable to effect this much with her benumbed and frozen fingers, and then she had to awaken her cousin in order to ask her for assistance. The latter, after Marie's death, and even during her lifetime, testified amply to these facts in her frequent and confidential conversations on the subject with Pere Albert. No one was in a position to give better testimony than this woman; for at that period she lived almost entirely with Marie, and they occupied the same bed at night. This person assured the father that upon such occasions, that though Marie struggled with all her might, every attempt to remain where she was proved useless; and, she added, that once or twice when she herself had tried to aid her in the contest, the sister was actually lifted out of her arms by some invisible power, and borne out of the room as easily and lightly as if she had been a wreath of straw.

The visits of the holy souls from Purgatory, though of course accompanied by the ineffable consolation of knowing they were safe, were yet in other ways as painful, or even more so, than were these demoniac visitations to Marie; seeing that they invariably entailed upon her a vast amount of extra suffering in order to their deliverance.

Her director seems to have by no means relied too weakly or implicitly on the truth of these spiritual communications with the inhabitants of Purgatory. He took, on the contrary, in the beginning, all possible precautions, and imposed all possible conditions on these ghostly visitors, with a view of testing the truth of their revelations, before permitting his penitent to undertake the good offices which they came imploring at her hands. The first time an apparition of this kind occurred, he refused absolutely to believe in its reality, and it was not until the poor suffering soul had appeared again and again to Marie, wearing her out by its sad looks and urgent pleadings, and forcing her in her own despite to apply again and again to the father for the necessary permission to relieve it, that he consented even to take the matter into consideration. When he had done so, he commanded Marie to test the truth of the vision and the real nature of the applicant by every possible touchstone which the Church has provided for such emergencies. In obedience to his orders, Marie commanded the spirit to light the blest candles which stood always upon her little altar, to make the sign of the cross, to pronounce first the sweet names of Jesus and Mary, and then at last that phrase which gathers the whole history of Our Lord's Divine and human generation into the sublimity of a single sentence, " The Word was made flesh and dwelt amongst us." All this the soul did, not only without hesitation, but with great and evident alacrity and joy, as Marie assured the father; nevertheless, it was not until the apparition actually occurred one day in his own presence, that he brought himself to make a decision in its favor.

The holy soul does not appear to have manifested itself actually to his bodily eyes on this occasion, but he saw all the outward results of its visit, the candles being lighted, while he and his companion were at a considerable distance from them, and every other command dictated by him to Marie obeyed in such a manner, as left no doubt on his mind as to its invisible presence in the chamber. Then, but not till then, he gave the permission for which she had so long been craving; and from that moment until the hour of her death, she may almost be said to have been plunged, body and soul, into Purgatory herself, by the constant state of suffering which the demands of its inhabitants for aid, entailed upon her. They were frequently souls with which she had been in intimate relation during the days of their earthly existence, or whose salvation, almost at the last hour of grace, had been effected, by her efforts, but multitudes visited her besides, whom she had never known or heard of before. Some of these holy sufferers told her ingenuously the nature of their chastisement, and the sin for which it was inflicted; others, not permitted, apparently, even the poor satisfaction of complaining, stood before her in all the mute eloquence of woe; saddening her heart by their looks of anguish, and compelling her to rack her brain in order to discover what, in the punishment of her own person, might prove their fitting remedy. And they came to her thus, not merely when she was in prayer in the Church or in her chamber, but at any hour of the night or day that it was permitted them to do so—waking her out of her scanty and hardly earned slumbers—saddening her moments of brief joy—and gazing on her even at her meals, until she could neither eat nor drink for very sorrow and sympathy in their woe.

One of the first who thus haunted her, and for whom she was called upon to suffer, was a man who had been rich in his lifetime, and of high consideration in the town; but who, unhappily for himself, had passed his days, like Dives, in feasting and disorder. The devil, who had contrived dexterously to blind him in his days of health, as to the real tendency of such a course, played off his last, and what is often his most successful manœuvre upon such souls, by showing it to him in its true colors at the hour of death, and so filling him with despair. Never did the enemy of souls seem more certain of success; never nearer to seizing on his prey than he was in the present instance. Neither the family nor friends of his unhappy victims; neither the priests nor religious called in to aid him, could succeed in calming his anguish, or in inducing him to consider, even for a moment, the possibility of his own salvation. Instead of the sweet names of Jesus and of Mary, that of his master, the devil, was continually on his lips. He raved of him night and day, saw him, as it almost seemed, actually with the very eyes of his body, and struck violently and abused any one who even ventured to hint, in his hearing, at that inexhaustible, mercy of God, which the tempter was whispering in his ear, he had forfeited for ever.

Marie's cousin chanced to know this man, and

hearing of the frightful state in which he was lying on his death-bed asked her to go and see what she could do to save him. She went at once, and at the door she saw visibly (as one can easily believe in such a case) a frightful demon, who, crying out, "What are you doing here? this man belongs to us;" tried by his fearful howls and threatening looks and gestures to terrify her from entering. But Marie was used to such demonstrations, and knew how to meet them. Passing him with the sign of the cross and a look of silent scorn, she made her way at once, and unbidden, to the chamber of his victim. He lay extended, apparently without the power of speech or hearing, on a bed; but she saw, as in a vision, that he was surrounded by seven demons, one of whom was whispering so continually in his ear, as effectually to prevent his attending to the pious suggestions of the friends who watched him still, in hopes of his ultimate conversion. At that awful sight, Marie fell upon her knees, and addressing herself more especially to the Blessed Virgin, the mother of mankind, and true refuge of the sinner, she offered herself to go security for the poor wretch before her, by taking upon herself the debt of suffering which his sinful life had entailed upon him, if only that he himself might be saved alive from hell.

After having thus, as she hoped, enlisted our sweet heavenly mother in his favor, she addressed the poor man himself, and though the demon at his pillow did all he could to hinder her, she persisted in her endeavors until she had compelled him, as it were, in his own despite, to listen to her words. Once in possession of his ear, she pleaded with him for his own soul, with an eloquence which only the Holy Ghost Himself could have poured out upon her lips. She told him that if his sins were as numerous as the sands of the sea, yet the mercies of God were more countless still, and that if, as he said, the jaws of hell were already gaping to receive him, the gates of Paradise, on the other hand, were equally ready to open to him at the first whisper of entreaty he might deign to offer. Jesus had died for sinners; he had then but to wash himself in the blood of Jesus, in order to cleanse his soul from sin. Mary had offered up Jesus for sinners; he had therefore but to address himself to her in order to receive anew the gift which she had already given to him and to all mankind, of a Saviour on Mount Calvary. Thus ringing the changes continually on the precious names of the Mother and the Son, Marie succeeded at last in forcing them through the thick mists in which the devil had enveloped the understanding of his predestined victim, and in depositing them in his heart.

Then, as in the days when Jesus spoke peace unto the waters, there followed a great calm! A deep sigh of relief burst from the bosom of the dying man; and from those whitened lips, which had hitherto breathed nought but blasphemy and despair, there fell distinctly, to the infinite astonishment of all who heard him, the sweet names of Jesus and of Mary. With those two words the victory was won—the devils fled before them!

Calmly and gently the man who, one short hour before, had been raving like a lunatic, now conferred with Sœur Marie on the condition of his soul; and listened in turn to her instructions and exhortations with the docile humility of a child. A priest was sent for to administer the last sacraments, and he departed this life a few days afterwards in a peace and joy which, to those who had seen him previously, appeared almost more wonderful than even the miraculous cure of his body would have been.

But he had left a friend, of whom they knew not, behind him to pay his ransom. Scarcely had he breathed his last, ere his "security," seized with a presentiment of what was coming, cried out in her anguish, that she should have to pay dearly for his salvation. Her cousin heard the words, and knowing from past experience that they were almost as certain as a prophecy, could not forbear both feeling and expressing some regret, that by her own interposition in favor of the sick man, she had brought this new martyrdom upon her. Contrary to her wont, Marie turned sharply round, and after rebuking her severely for her want of zeal, she ended by declaring that she herself was ready to accept all of suffering that a human creature was capable of enduring for the sake of saving but a single soul.

Even as she was speaking these words of burning charity, her martyrdom had begun. The sinner whom she had just been attending on his death-bed appeared bodily before her. For six weeks afterwards he visited her constantly, gazing on her in a wordless anguish more eloquent than words themselves; and during all that time, Marie endured a very martyrdom of woe on his account.

It was, as she herself described it, as if she were

being cut and wounded, all over the body, by unseen razors. Sometimes she burned as with a raging fever, at others she shivered with a sensation as if cold water were dropping continually upon her, and freezing into icicles as it touched her person. With a fierce and irrepressible hunger she felt such an intolerable disgust for nourishment, that for eight successive days she could not swallow even a single morsel of solid food; and the little liquid with which she supported life, no matter what its real nature might be, became so intensely bitter as it touched her lips, that the pain of drinking was even more insupportable than the desire to do so, by which it had been preceded. All this Marie endured with great spiritual joy and patience; albeit the mere fact of bodily pain often forced cries of agony from her lips, and such abundance of tears from her eyes, that those who beheld her thus, were compelled in pure pity to weep along with her. In the midst of this terrible anguish she was strengthened and consoled by a vision of the Blessed Virgin and the Divine Child, accompanied by St. Joseph and her own St. Albert; and she was given at the same time to understand that the man on whose account she was undergoing penance owed his salvation entirely to

Mary, for whom in the midst of his disordered life he had always retained a certain amount of tenderness and devotion. Shortly after this, the soul appeared to her again and spoke. She tested the real nature of the apparition by commanding it to pronounce the words of the gospel, *Verbum caro factum est*; and having gladly complied with this request, he thanked her, in a very humble and touching manner, for all she had done to save him, assuring her, that at the very moment when she had succeeded in infusing a gleam of hope into his soul, he had seen, almost as it were with the eyes of his body, the demons in crowds preparing joyfully to drag him down with them into hell. Afterwards he explained to her that he had not been permitted to speak to her before, in punishment of the evil use to which in his lifetime he had applied the gift of speech, devoting it to the offence alike of God and man, by blaspheming, swearing, perjury, and detraction, and he revealed to her, at the same time, both the cause and nature of the suffering she was enduring on his account. That craving for food, and disgust and impossibility of taking it, was a part of the satisfaction which he owed for the gluttony and debauchery of his previous existence; that laceration, as if by razors, with fever and alternate freezing, were the payments, in part at least, for his offences against purity. She suffered in her limbs, because of his passionate impatience during a somewhat similar affliction in his lifetime; in her hands, because his had been closed obdurately to the needy and unfortunate: in her whole person, and even, as it were, to the very marrow of her bones, because of the self-love and self-indulgence in which he had so saturated his being, that, from first to last, the ease and pleasure of his body had been the only real thing he lived for, the one sole end and aim of his existence. He told her the number of years for which he was condemned to Purgatory, speaking of his suffering there with a kind of fierce and eager joy, as being the means whereby his soul was to be cleansed and fitted for the eternal vision of its Creator, and acknowledging that, terrible as they no doubt were, they were yet too little for the life of sin of which they were the just chastisement. But the love and longing for God was upon him even then, and overpowered him; and while in the very act of avowing the over-mercifulness of his probation, he could not forbear entreating her to persevere in the pains and mortifications by which alone it could be shortened.

From that time he was hardly ever absent a moment from her side, thanking her for all she was enduring on his account, encouraging her in her bitter anguish by the assurance that every pain she suffered took so much from the length of his sentence, and complaining (poor soul!) sadly, but yet resignedly, of the cruelty of his own family and former friends, who, having inherited all his good things, left him neglected and forgotten in his burning prison. At length, on the 25th of March, the especial Feast of Our Blessed Lady, to whom he owed so especially his salvation, he appeared for the last time to Marie, full of joy and gratitude, to announce to her that her long and bitter penance on his account was ended, and that he was about immediately to enter heaven, where he would never cease to remember her and all those who had been instrumental, through her means, in shortening his purgation, most affectionately before the throne of God.

It would be well if we reflected seriously on this history. First, for the sake of our dead friends. We are all perhaps too apt to canonise those whom we have loved and lost for ever, thus softening unconsciously our own affliction by embalming their memories amid the joys of Paradise; or, if we do not entirely fall into this weakness, we yet dismiss them, after a few weeks or months of prayer, after a few Masses, more or less, said for them, from our minds, little knowing, little dreaming from what long years of anguish a greater diligence on our parts might possibly have saved them.

And, in the next place, we should consider it for our own,—we who sin small sins so easily,—we who talk so lightly, so playfully, even of Purgatory; saying, some of us at all events, either from real indifference, or from humility, which is false, if it is not feigned—" Oh, as to Purgatory if I can only get there, I shall be quite contented"—never reflecting on the terrible evil of sin which brings us there, or upon the awful nature of those cleansing fires whereby men suffer without merit more a thousand times than they would do by the worst penance they could inflict (with the addition of its merit) upon their own bodies in this world. So long as punishment is not eternal, we are apt to think lightly of it; and perhaps God, in His loving tenderness for His creatures, has sometimes permitted these visitations of the holy souls to their brethren still existing in the flesh, for no other reason than to teach us not to esteem too lightly, as we so often do, (if indeed we forget them not altogether,) the penalties we are day by day laying up for ourselves in another world by our careless habitudes of sin in this one.

The story of this poor soul in Purgatory, which I have given as an example, is only one among many others in Sœur Marie's life as well authenticated as such things can be, her director having been most rigid in the examination of all that portion of her life which touched upon the supernatural, and having, so far from relying implicitly upon his own judgment, consulted and compelled her to consult, various learned fathers, (chiefly of the Society of Jesus,) who were all unanimously of opinion that in her case there was no delusion, she being evidently one of those chosen souls set apart by God from time to time to do great things for His service, both in regard to their brethren still existing in the flesh, and to those who, having departed out of the body, are blest and pardoned, and yet suffering still—the holy souls in Purgatory!

The fact, indeed, became so patent at last to all who knew her, that people began to look upon the success of her prayers as certain, and to flock to her, as a matter of course, upon all occasions where their difficulties, whether spiritual or temporal, seemed to call for unusual aid. The richest, the wisest, the most powerful inhabitants of Liege, and of the country for leagues around it, came to her for advice, revealing the sins and secrets of their lives with as much candor and confidence as they would have done to their director; and she met their advances with such grace and bounty, and put so much tact and wisdom into her mode of hearing and answering their strange communications, that, simple and ignorant of all human learning as they knew her to be, no one ever left her without feeling that they had acquired something for future guidance or consolation by the interview, of which they had previously been ignorant. People wrote to her when they were unable to consult her personally, and her answers, though often incorrect in language, are models as to sense, of spiritual modesty and wisdom. Not that she made any pretence to learning, for in her correspondence, as in her conversation, she was simplicity itself. A smiling, kindly face, winning all hearts by the sweet modesty of its expression; a clear and unaffected choice of words, accompanied by a genuine sympathy in the anxieties of the persons consulting her—these, with the holy aspirations and ejaculatory prayers with which, in her burning fervor, she mingled all she said or did, were her only means of convincing or consoling others, and these proved always, or almost always, more than sufficient for the purpose.

Her advice was always good; often it was founded upon such a strange and preternatural knowledge of the peculiar circumstances of the case, that it was impossible to doubt of its having been given under a direct inspiration of the Holy Ghost Himself. How indeed could it have been otherwise? She was always, under all circumstances, and in whatever company she found herself, in a state of habitual recollection of God's presence. He was ever with her in her thoughts; how then could He ever be long absent from her discourse? She was ever conversing with Him in the secret of her own soul; how then could He ever refuse her the little wisdom needed for the comfort of His creatures, when charity compelled her to address herself to them? Is there not, moreover, an especial privilege attached to innocence? And if Marie saw and judged of many things with a wisdom and clearness of which neither her sex nor her natural faculties in themselves were capable, may it not have been because she saw and judged them by the light of God's brightness indwelling in her spirit by virtue of that especial promise of Our Lord, which, if in its totality of enjoyment it be reserved for heaven, is yet often partially bestowed upon earth on those who, like Marie, live as the angels live, free from the trammels of the flesh, from the cradle to the grave. Surely it was of these, the lilies of His earthly kingdom, that Jesus said, "Blessed are the clean of heart, for they shall see God."

CHAPTER X.

Dealing with Sœur Marie as He deals often with His most favored servants, God seems to have intended that in her person, even bodily ailments should be a matter of self-election rather than of compulsion; and for this end, He offered her more than once her choice between suffering and consolation; condescending even to assure her, in order that her free will might be absolutely unimpaired in the election, that it would be in no wise displeasing to Him if she should chance to prefer the latter. But, like all those who have been perfect enough to be thus left to the desires of their own hearts, Marie resolutely put aside the proffered crown of roses, to take up that which, thorn-woven as it was, had yet been made sweet and precious to her soul by the fact of its having once pressed upon the brow of Jesus, and her answer, like that of all the saints, was still the same, "I desire, O my God, but two things in this world; to suffer and to love."

And this desire was no transitory wish, no

vague and undefined sentiment, such as the weakest souls occasionally feel in some chance hour of fervor.

In such moods, they ask for suffering, and fancy they desire it, but when the reality of the wish is tested, and the feeble prayer even partially granted, they shrink back repining. The lightest touch of the very cross they prayed for, seems too much for calm endurance, and God, in pure pity for their weakness, often then withdraws it altogether from their shoulders, and leaves them to the spiritual mediocrity they have, in a manner, chosen for themselves. The desire of Marie's soul, on the contrary, was that strong, true desire of a strong, true nature, which infallibly attracts the pressure of the hand of God; that loving hand which only strikes to heal, only offers the cross to the acceptance of His creatures, in order that hereafter it may become their crown.

The most bitter of Marie's bitter trials were undoubtedly those laid upon her either for the conversion of a sinner, or for the relief of a holy soul in Purgatory, such trials being invariably accompanied by something of that mental dereliction which lifts the woes of Gethsemani to almost a level with the anguish of Mount Calvary; whereas she seemed raised above herself by a certain sublime sense of joy, whenever she was made to understand that any specified and especial suffering, mental as well as bodily, had been given to her for no other end than to render her, in all ways possible, a more perfect pattern and likeness of her crucified Spouse.

Of suffering such as this she never could have enough, and suffering increased with love, and love fed and grew on suffering, until her desire for it became insatiable, and at the slightest decrease of the outward pressure—the smallest return to health or comfort—she was ready to cry out with the holy solitary of the desert, "Hast Thou then quite forgotten me, O my God? or have I offended Thee? that Thou dost visit me no more!"

There were days in which she was so filled and transported out of herself by those sufferings of love, and this love of suffering, that the bare mention of the name of Jesus was sufficient to throw her into an ecstasy, and her cousin knowing this, once took advantage of the circumstance to ask her with a little innocent malice, as if she herself were not quite certain of the fact, whether she really and truly loved Him. "Dost thou hear, O my God?" cried the sister—instantly grasping her little crucifix. "They ask me if I love Thee! If I love Thee, O my Jesus—if I love Thee! Yes, yes! I love Thee! More than myself, more than the whole world, and I would love Thee all by myself, more than all the rest of Thy creatures put together, if I could. I love Thee, and would quit all to love Thee better—leave all in order more perfectly to embrace Thee—renounce all in order more profoundly to adore Thee—and my only grief and shame is the time which I have hitherto misspent unloving Thee and unladen with Thy cross!"

Once, on the feast of St. Francis Xavier, for whom from her childhood she had always felt the tenderest devotion, being at prayer in her little chamber and occupied in devout consideration of the wonders of his life, she was seized with such a holy envy of the fatigues and sufferings and martyrdoms which he and his saintly followers had braved and borne for the conversion of the heathen, that she could hardly forbear repining at the fact, that by her lot in life she was necessarily debarred from all participations in such labor. Then softly and seriously, in a voice from heaven, came the answer to her thoughts: "The martyrdoms of Japan and China, O my daughter, were not meant for children, but the martyrdoms of Liege, on the contrary, will be always within your reach." But Marie, in her childlike simplicity, replied, "Saint and dear father, tell me, I beseech you, of what martyrdoms are you speaking now?" And again the voice answered gently, "They are everywhere, and can be found by all who truly seek them, for they consist in affronts and persecutions and calumnies endured meekly for the sake of Jesus—and in sufferings and sorrows borne willingly for His love!"

Oh, wise and gracious words of a wise and gracious saint! Would that we could each of us in the daily petty martyrdoms of our existence take them seriously to heart. For he meant, no doubt, and no doubt Sœur Marie understood him so to mean, that we may each of us, if we will, find martyrdoms sufficient to secure salvation in the calm endurance of the hundred nameless causes of sorrows or annoyance which lie scattered everywhere over the path of life, and which so far from accepting and cherishing as a means of merit, we too often adulterate into sin by the impatience and vexation of spirit wherewith, unfortunately for ourselves, we meet them.

Marie's love of suffering naturally made her love the cross; its outward symbol, and her love of the cross was such, that consciously or unconsciously, she continually reproduced its image in the course of her daily labors. She made the sign of the cross upon everything she saw or touched, and before even the most trivial of her actions. She prostrated ever before the cross, and prayed often when alone, with her arms extended in its likeness. Even in trifles regarding her household occupations, she could not forget it, the very sticks with which she laid the fire assumed, somehow or other, in her hands the form of a cross, and she used to say, in her innocent, smiling manner, that if she were rich enough to choose, she would never employ herself upon any work of which the pattern did not recall it to her mind. The feast of the exaltation of the cross was consequently one of the greatest of the year for her. The gray light of morning had hardly dawned upon the city ere she was on foot, preparing, with something of that yearning tenderness which the holy women must have felt as they journeyed towards the sepulchre, to salute and adore the relic of the true cross, preserved in the collegiate church of the holy cross at Liege, and exhibited on that day to the veneration of the faithful.

Prostrate in spirit, she there adored it as if it

were still standing on Mount Calvary, and still wet with the blood of her Divine Spouse, and the day was nearly spent ere she even thought of returning homewards. Then more than once it happened, that the long hours spent in this loving adoration were rewarded by a vision in which a grievously heavy cross seemed to be laid upon her shoulders. The pain was excessive, and the weight almost more than she felt that she could endure; nevertheless, her whole soul trembled with joy at the idea that she was thus loaded in resemblance to her Lord, and instead of yielding to the natural feeling which might have sent her home by the shortest road, she invariably chose the longest and most difficult, climbing the steep weary hill she had thus to traverse, in the sweet and loving persuasion that she was mounting with Jesus up to Calvary, and aiding Him, in spirit at least, like Simon, in the carriage of His cross. Occasionally her visions took another guise, but they all tended to the same end, namely, to satisfy and increase her love and devotion to the cross. Sometimes Jesus Himself appeared to her in the likeness of a child, bearing a pannier of little crosses in His hand; at others, a shower of crosses, small and large, emblematic of future suffering, were rained down upon her; and when her heart still cried out for more, her Divine Spouse Himself, in a separate gracious vision, deigned to name her, "Sœur Marie Albert of the Cross of Jesus"—a title which she retained jealously to death, and which Père Albert caused to be engraved, as her only real claim to honor, on her tombstone afterwards.

Once, on a certain day in the year of Our Lord 1669, being about to receive holy communion, she heard the voice of her holy father, St Albert, thus addressing itself to her soul:—

"Courage, little sister, courage! for your Divine Spouse is about to enter into your soul, not to anoint it with peace and joy, but to load it on the contrary with all the sorrows of Mount Calvary. He will bring with Him the nails that pierced Him, the thorns that crowned Him, the thongs that tore His innocent flesh, and the sadness and desolation with which His soul was deluged. Courage, therefore, courage! Love and suffer yet a little longer here. Eternity will surely be long enough for joy. Suffer while you may, for only in this life can you do so with merit. It was given to you for no other purpose, and without suffering, the gift would be unworthy of your acceptance."

Suffering predicted by that heavenly voice was never long in making its appearance. It came to her from all varieties of causes, even at the moment when it was least expected, and generally in the precise form in which, at the time being, it seemed the most intolerable and impossible of endurance.

Sometimes, as we have said before, it was the devil who tried, in all sorts of saintly and human disguises, to betray her soul, now tempting her to excessive penance, now to undue indulgence; but ever, in spite of himself, betraying his real nature by the efforts which he made to withdraw her from the obedience she owed and had vowed to her director.

Often, her bodily maladies were made worse to endure than pain itself, by the mental anguish with which they were accompanied. Sadness, fear, anxiety, reluctance, all the various moods of sorrow which Our Divine Lord endured for us in the garden were hers by turn, and after that, and worse by far, to a soul in love like hers with innocence, came the temptation to commit sin.

She was naturally of a most sweet and patient temperament, and hardly even capable of being moved to anger, excepting when, like her Divine

Lord, a holy zeal for God's wounded honor roused her to heroic indignation; nevertheless, for a short period of her life, her whole nature seemed to change within her, and who she had hitherto been accustomed to receive insults with a smiling face, and to suffer even blows without remonstrance, found herself all of a sudden, moved to feelings of vexation at the merest trifles or the most reasonable and gently expressed contradiction. A look or gesture roused her, a single word disturbed her, and for the time being, peace seemed utterly to forsake her and to leave storm and tumult in her soul instead. But the storm might rage as it would, it never was allowed external utterance, and the waves of anger, however high they rose, were never permitted to overflow the boundaries which reason and religion set them.

Marie had learned long ago to recognize the fact of the twofold nature which we all have within us; and now, more than ever, she strove to apply the lesson by compelling the lower portion of her being to obey the higher, or in her own pithy and expressive language, by making "Marie Sellier" submit in all things to "Sœur Marie Albert of the Cross of Jesus," as to her just and lawfully appointed superior. So perfectly, in fact, was that submission rendered, that no one, however intimate with her, could ever detect, in her outward conduct, any trace of the fiery trial which raged within. The persons who had most excited her temper, were left in absolute ignorance of their having done so, a fact which never prevented her going at once to her director to reveal the temptation with many tears, and to demand and obtain such a meed of penance and reprimand, as perhaps he would never have ventured to award, if she had been really guilty of the transgression she avowed. But a yet more severe trial was to assail her still, in a fierce temptation against the virtue of the angels. It is true, the combat was not of long duration, but it was terrible while it lasted. Blood gushed from her nostrils, and as once happened to St. Francis Xavier, burst in big drops from every pore in her body, but faint and exhausted as nature might be, her soul still triumphed over the ememies of its purity, and kept them at a distance, and then at last her constancy was rewarded. The queen of angels, the virgin of all virgins, came herself, accompanied by St. Albert, to her assistance, and instantly the combat ceased. Yet more, our blessed mother, with all the tender lovingness of a human mother, wiped from the face of the exhausted girl the bloody tears which were pouring down it, promised gently that she should never again be assailed in a similar manner, and that she should be restored, moreover, to her primitive ignorance (for innocence she had never lost) as to the real nature of the vice upon which she had been tempted, and bound her waist, as a pledge and token of the fulfillment of that promise, with a girdle brilliant as if set in diamonds.

Afterwards she laid the Divine Child upon Marie's bosom, beseeching Him to take her for His spouse, and Jesus graciously assented; but even while laying His hand upon her head, and promising that she should be His own for ever, He forgot not, like a wise and gentle master, to urge the value of suffering upon her soul, exhorting her to finish as she had begun, and to continue to endure bravely and generously even to the very end. Then He gave her His benediction, and the vision both of mother and child instantly departed from her.

In consequence of this heavenly gift, Marie often afterwards, at the instance of her director, made other similar girdles, to be given to persons suffering under the temptation from which it had delivered her, and they proved, as he declares, invariably efficacious for the purpose. Among others, a holy Carmelite father, who on this account had solicited the prayers of Marie, though without specifying the precise nature of his needs, was completely delivered from his trouble, by a girdle which Pere Albert had caused her to make, and which he then sent to him, as a New Year's gift. Not content in thanking Marie in a letter addressed to herself, this good father wrote also to Pere Albert, declaring more specifically the nature of the grace he had received, and protesting his belief that it was owing, and must be attributed wholly and entirely, to the merits and prayers of his "little sister in Jesus Christ," seeing that he had already asked his deliverance, and caused it to be asked by others, not once only, but a thousand times in vain. He ended his letter, in a very humble and touching manner, by giving thanks to God, for that He had hidden His secrets from the wise and learned, to reveal them to the simple, adding a formal declaration to the effect, that he had written this account of his spiritual malady and its cure solely for the sake of giving due glory to God, and honor to the poor girl, by whom his deliverance had been effected. This letter, containing, as it did, such gravely conscientious matter, was naturally kept secret during the lifetimes of those it principally concerned, but it was included by Père Albert in the MS. biography, which he compiled, of Sœur Marie after her death. In giving this and similar accounts, he adds, with his wonted prudence and candor, that he does not pretend to decide whether the effect produced by these girdles really proceeded from their being miraculous, or whether they were chiefly owing to the prayers and good works of her who made them. Possibly it was the two combined together, united (if we may venture to suggest a third ingredient) to the humility of those who, in asking or accepting of such a gift, acknowledged openly and generously to the infirmity of their nature.

From whatever cause Marie's sufferings arose, whether from the natural ailments or the voluntary chastisement of the body, whether from sadness of mind, or temptation, or the persecution of her human brethren, they were no doubt frequently accompanied and made endurable by great and supernatural consolations, the holy fathers being all unanimously of opinion that spiritual joy is usually measured out in proportion to sorrow, and that Christ, in such cases, shows Himself at once the thief and the good Samaritan of the gospel, pouring the healing balm of comfort into the very wounds which He Himself, for His own loving ends, has inflicted on His creatures. But let those who love Him, or who long at least to love Him, beware of asking or of even wishing for this celestial remedy, this precious mingling of the olive and the vine, tending as it might do, perhaps to the too complete and rapid healing of their heart-wounds. Let them leave themselves generously in His hands, " without a yea, and without a nay," as the loving St. Francis has it, and they may rest assured, that even while He seems to be trying their strength to the utmost, He is still, like a good physician, watchful of their weakness, ready, at the first symptoms of sinking on their part, to take the cross from their shoulders, and to lay it once more (O sweet and loving Jesus, how miserably we requite Thy kindness!) on His own.

Thus it was that He watched Sœur Marie, testing at once her strength and weakness, when the moment came at last, when He judged that He might safely impose upon her the cross which he has reserved more especially for His saints, and which is at once the result of sanctity, and its culminating point—the cross of life itself.

No one can love as the saints have loved, without longing to behold the object so beloved, and this longing, and this desire, growing and increasing with every hour of delay, becomes at last such a martyrdom of joy and sorrow, as that, if it were not regulated by the loving hand which sends it, no creature could endure it and still live on.

It is the greatest, often perhaps the only, suffering of the holy souls in Purgatory, who, even with the knowledge that it must one day end for them in gladness, find in it sufficient penance for the sins and failings of a lifetime; what, then, must it be to a soul still hampered with the burthen of a flesh, still weighed down by the necessity of condescending to its needs, still condemned to crawl with it on earth, while trembling and all on fire with love, it poises its eager wings, ready, as far as a creature ever can be ready, to soar at once and for ever to the bosom of its God! The germ of this desire had, no doubt, been in Sœur Marie's soul from childhood, and it grew with her growth, and increased with the fervor of increasing years, until it seemed to her at last as a sort of necessity to die; and then, when she was in the midst of the love and gladness of this thought, St. Albert, in a vision, bade her ask for the prolongation of that life which she was so panting to lay down, in order that it might still, in this martyrdom of love, win souls for the heart of Jesus. At first she hesitated, not so much because of the unutterable anguish to her soul of such a prayer, as because of the obedience which she had vowed to her director, and which she feared she might infringe upon, if she made a petition of such importance without his express permission. St. Albert had ever encouraged her in this spirit of obedience, and had taught her upon all such occasions to prefer the counsels of the visible guide whom God had given her to those even of very saints themselves, because, as he said, and as she knew full well already, in the one there was always certainty, whereas in the other, as in all that occurred in visions, there was a possibility of self-delusion. Now then he admitted her objections, and having first, by his permission, declared that she only intended this petition for life in as far as it it might be approved of by her director, she repeated and wrote down the following words:—

"O my Jesus, I, the least and most unworthy of thy servant, do beseech Thee in all humility to prolong my life, in order that I may suffer still for the conversion of sinners, and for the ease and deliverance of the holy souls in Purgatory!"

Scarcely had she said the words, ere she felt that her petition had been accepted, and that a cross, heavier far than any she had ever borne before, was being laid upon her shoulders. But it was a true cross of the saint at last,—the cross of the strong, eager soul burning with desire to behold its God,— the cross which St. Theresa bore when she faltered forth that tender loving plaint, which happily finds an echo still in many a tender, loving, living heart; that "she was dying because she could not die,"— the cross, in fine, which St. Paul carried on his shoulders, at the moment when, unable to bear its mingled pain and ecstacy in silence any longer, he published to the whole Christian world his conviction that death were better far—his desire "to be dissolved, and to be with Christ."

That cross was upon Marie's shoulders now,— that desire was in her heart,—and whatever she had felt before of yearnings for eternity, seemed but as the first flutterings of the eaglet in its nest, compared to the long grand sweep with which afterwards in its full strength of wing, it soars upwards to the sun!

She lived full thirty years after this gift of life so reluctantly asked for, so heroically accepted; and during all that time she bore its pain without failing or faltering for a moment, going about her common daily duties, as well as fulfilling those which were more important, not too great for the one, or too little for the other, never complaining, never gloomy, meek and silent as a wounded dove, hiding the arrow in her heart beneath an unruffled exterior and a smiling face, waiting and waiting still in her great patience until the due number of souls appointed to her mission had been safely sent on before her, ere she herself laid down the burthen of this life and went to join them in eternity!

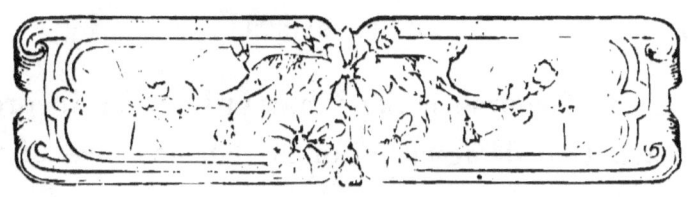

CHAPTER XI.

Saints have died ere now of the love of God by a foretaste of His sweetness—martyrs in the soul,—just as saints have died for His love, by a profession of the true faith before His enemies—martyrs in the body. It hardly seems to me too much to assume that by an especial privilege it was given to the humble creature, whose hidden life I have been endeavoring imperfectly to trace out, to share in her measure and degree in the separate merits and sanctifications of each of these several modes of martyrdom. Not a day for thirty years upon which she might not have said, with her great mother St. Theresa, that she was dying because she could not die, and at the close of that long period of endurance, it was from the hand of an assassin that she received the boon, so long desired and so long delayed, of death—death, which, in the language and the sentiments of the saints, is but another and more human word for the gift of eternal life. Simply a murder does not of course make a martyrdom, for in order to reach that designation in the heroic sense of the word, it must have been a murder consequent upon some act or outspoken sentiment whereby God's glory has been vindicated, or His interests defended against the attacks and aspersions of His foes. Tried by this test, the assault which in the end hastened Marie to the tomb may well be styled a martyrdom, seeing that it was planned and executed by certain men who, having been frustrated by her charitable interference in their designs against innocence, resolved to wreak their disappointment upon her. Murder in those wild times was much easier of accomplishment than it is at present; for albeit the law fell heavily enough upon the offender whenever it could discover him, it had not yet arrived at that higher wisdom which looks rather to the prevention of crime by means of a strong and well organized police, than even to its just punishment after once it has been committed. Liege was a mercantile and crowded city, artisans of the lowest class were employed in great numbers in its mines and workshops; strangers of all grades and nations flocked in continually for the purposes of commerce; the city guard was small and ineffective in comparison with the population it was intended to protect; and the streets of the town, moreover, huddled and crowded together, (as they are in all old cities,) afforded all sorts of nooks and corners where the assassin could lurk unseen, until the precise moment in which he considered it safe to spring upon his prey. Murder under circumstances such as these was no uncommon thing even in the broad daylight, the rich and powerful being quite as often the object of the assassin's knife, probably indeed oftener, than the poor and unprotected. But feeble and defenceless as Sœur Marie was, she had nevertheless a buckler of strength of which the great ones of the town were destitute, and the very men who had planned her murder yet hesitated to strike her openly, knowing as they did, that the poor of the city would rise as a single man in defence of her whom they so justly styled their mother. Like Judas, therefore, they were compelled to wait until even-tide, in order to effect their treachery with due safety to themselves. It was no very difficult matter after all, for Marie never had the respite of a day's health which she did not employ in the service of the poor, coming and going continually through the town, and always beginning and ending the day by prayers in the Church nearest to the point to which her pious labor called her. They had but to ascertain, accordingly, the quarter of the town she would visit in the morning, in order to make sure of the church she was most likely to stop at on her way home at night. Quite unconscious or regardless of the plot against her, she was returning one evening from the Church of St. Remi, where she had finished her day by prayer, and was passing through a long lonely passage, behind that of St. Paul, when a large stone, aimed at her by one of these miscreants, hit her exactly on the temples.

Deluged in her own blood, she fell senseless to the ground, and fancying they had accomplished their purpose, her would-be assassins quietly retired. Had she shown any sign of life at the moment, they would probably have repeated their blows, until they had extinguished it altogether; but as it was, she only recovered her senses after their departure, and then either managed to crawl home herself, or being discovered in that condition, was carried there by her friends. The surgeon who was immediately called in to attend her for the injury, declared it to be a mystery to him how such a blow, from the size of the stone, and the vital direction it had taken, had not killed her on the spot. It had not killed her certainly, but it proved, for all that, her death-blow, for she never entirely rallied from the long and dangerous illness which followed its infliction. For some months, indeed, after her partial recovery, she continued to drag herself about as best she could to her ordinary work of mercy, but day by day she grew more feeble and more unequal to the effort. Dropsy, the life-long malady of her constitution, finally set in, and she took to her bed at last, never to rise from it again! There, during all the varying phases of one of the most wearisome and trying maladies to which the human frame is subject, she might be seen, giving, in her own person, a faithful rendering of those lessons of patience and humility which she had so often proffered by word of mouth to others. She knew well the persons of the men who had helped, indirectly, by their evil designs against her, to lay her on that bed of anguish, but she would never name them even to her director, saying that as she had pardoned them from her heart of hearts, she had no desire to see them either punished by the law, or to inflict punishment herself upon them by thus giving up their names to public execration.

Probably, indeed, Sœur Marie did even more than pradon them; probably, in her secret soul, she thanked them for having shortened the weary hours of her exile, which, but for that well-directed blow, might have still, to all appearances, lasted for years. For many months she continued thus to fluctuate between life and death;-the latter quietly and steadily approaching, the former as quietly and steadily receding, and she herself, the object of the combat, showing, as a very angel in peace, in tranquility and resignation to all who had the privilege of approaching her on her death-bead. By the look of ineffable peace upon her brow, by the gentle smile for ever playing on her pale lips, she made of that death-bed a very pulpit from whence, without uttering a single syllable, she preached continually to their souls; and when they beheld the atmosphere of perpetual calmness in which she rested, they could hardly believe in the reality of the pains which, nevertheless, they were well aware she must be enduring. Still less did they dream of the mental anguish which, at the same time, wrung her soul, occupied incessantly, as her confessor assures us that she was, in contemplation on Mount Calvary, and drowned and absorbed in the sufferings of its Divine Victim. The passion of her Divine Spouse grew, in fact, to be more than ever the sole object of her thoughts and aspirations during the protracted agonies of her last illness, and the crucifix, its best exponent, was forever in her hand, for not even in the forgetfulness of her short and restless slumbers did she ever let it go. To look upon the likeness of her dying Lord was her only recreation; to suffer with, and like Him, her only joy; and to die, as He had done, alone and abandoned of mankind, soon became the sole object of her ambition. Whenever Pere Albert visited her, he found her thus, hidden, as it were, in the wounds of Jesus, and holding sweet colloquies with Him upon all His sufferings, but never even alluding or hinting at her own. She considered Him especially as "the Man of sorrow, afflicted for our iniquities, and smitten for our sins;" atoning, by sufferings in every portion of His body, and in every faculty of His soul and senses, for the guilty indulgences which we have given to ours.

She saw Him, lonely and desolate, weeping in the garden—lonely and desolate, dying on the cross— the men for whose guilty sakes He had clothed Himself with sin, as with a garment, mocking at his misery: and God whose justice He was contenting by that all perfect holocaust filling up the appointed measure of His anguish by leaving Him to that same dereliction and loss of sense of the Divine Presence, which is at once the chief pain of Purgatory, and the final agony and despair of hell.

Human nature must infallibly have given way and perished in this double agony of body and soul, if it had not been miraculously supported; sometimes by bright and glorious visitations of the saints and angels; sometimes, and still more efficaciously, by a miraculous participation in the Body and Blood of Him whose sorrows she had thus made so entirely her own. Instances of such miraculous communions are often to be found in the lives of many others of the saints of God, and Pere Albert gives many good and solid reasons why they should have been more than usually frequent in that of Sœur Marie.

Hidden Sanctity seemed marked out as especially her vocation. It had been the one prayar of her life, ever since God had begun to work miraculously in her soul, that His gifts should be kept hidden from the world around her ; and with this same end in view she had exacted from all her confessors a promise of as much secrecy as to any revelations they compelled her to make of her interior state, as they would have been bound to observe, had it been a question of sin. Hitherto she had had her wish, and to the world at large she was merely known as an exceedingly pious person, addicted more than was usual in her own or in any other state of life to works of charity; no one who regarded her life merely on the surface ever even dreaming of the treasures of grace and the miraculous gifts which lay hidden underneath.

One evidence of her sanctity could not, indeed, be entirely concealed from the eyes of others, and this was the practice of daily communion, which her director not only permitted, but even, when her humility at times induced her to hesitate, enforced upon her by virtue of the obedience which she owed him. Her great devotion seemed to require this privilege, the purity of her life deserved it, her evident vocation to high sanctity appeared naturally to include this, the highest act of sanctity that a creature can perform, and the extraordinary suffering, mental and bodily, by which only such a vocation as hers can be successfully worked out, inevitably demanded in exchange all that extra strength and consolation, which can be found nowhere so abundantly as by direct contact and communication with Our Divine Lord, in the sacrament of His love. As long, however, as she was able to crawl to church and to assist at the Mass of dawn, she could indulge in this holy practice without exciting much comment or observation, but the moment she was prostrated on a bed of sickness, the thing became more difficult. It was the custom—custom which no one, however high in the church, or however holy, would have ventured to intermit—to carry the Blessed Sacrament openly and in procession, and with all the ceremonies prescribed by the Church to be observed upon such occasions, to the bedside of the dying; so that, if Pere Albert had decided upon thus administering his saintly penitent, in less than a week it would have been known all over Liege that Marie Sellier, the charitable *lingere*, was in the habit of receiving holy communion daily. Now, daily communion was unfortunately a very unfrequent practice in those days, men and women even, who are now canonised saints upon the altars of the Church, having been sometimes refused it by their directors, partly from personal doubts as to its propriety, but chiefly, as I believe, from undue deference to the state of public opinion on the subject.

If, consequently, it had become generally known that Père Albert had permitted it to Marie, one or other of these two things must inevitably have followed,—either the Liegois would have proclaimed her a saint, thus at once endangering her humility and grieving it, or (which was more likely still) they would have pronounced her a hypocrite, and made such an outcry both against her and her director, as would in the end have compelled the latter to withdraw the privilege altogether. For all these reasons, evidently wise and well-considered ones, Pert Albert tells us he was compelled reluctantly to deprive his penitent of daily communion whenever her long and grievous maladies prevented her seeking it at the church itself; and she submitted to this, the greatest to her of all privations, in the same spirit of submission and self-sacrifice, in which she accepted of less grievous trials. Then it was that Almighty God, ever more merciful than man, seeing at once the needs and the submission of His little handmaid, stepped in to aid her by those miraculous communions of which I have already spoken, and which were accorded to her, not merely during the period of her last illness, but in most of the long and grievous maladies by which that illness had been preceded. Sometimes it was given to her by the hand of an angel, sometimes by those of St. Albert, or of others, her patron saints and protectors, sometimes the Host itself, suspended above her head in a cloud of glory, descended softly and gently of its own accord, and laid itself on her lips.

Of the latter fact, Marie's cousin, upon whose word Pere Albert considered that he could implicity rely, had once, at least, if not oftener, actual ocular demonstration; for perceiving the invalid to open her mouth, and fancying it was in consequence of the burning thirst by which she was continually tormented, she was about to offer her some refreshment, when an invisible power seemed to withold her hand, and considering the sick woman more attentively, she perceived the sacred host lying on her tongue, parched, black, and swollen as it was with the only bodily suffering of which Jesus ever openly complained. Marie swallowed it almost directly afterwards and entered at once into an ecstatic trance, which lasted for many hours, and during which she remained, as was usual with her on such occasions, fixed, rigid and motionless as if she had been a statue. Upon one particular and most memorable occasion, Our Divine Lord deigned Himself to appear and communicate His spouse, after which He withdrew her heart, as it seemed to her, from her bosom, in order to imprint upon it the appearance of the instruments of His passion. He showed Himself in this vision of the natural height of man, majestic, and yet sweet and gracious beyond expression, and when He took her heart, it seemed to leave her bosom under the appearance of a little ball of fire.

Thus she remained till mid-day, languishing and dying, as it were, in the sweetness of that delicious robbery, her face beautiful as an angel's, her soul so rapt and absorbed in the ecstacy which held it, that the body well-nigh fainted away for lack of its companion, all its senses failing, and her voice, when she tried to speak, being soft and feeble as that of a little child. State of unutterable joy and of unutterable anguish, who shall conceive it or describe it! The sight, in that vision, of the nails, the scourges and the thorns whereby her beloved had suffered for her—the knowledge that He had now chosen her to bear them engraven upon her heart of hearts, thrilled her whole being with rushes alternatively of grief and of sacred gladness, and kindled within her such a vehement desire to suffer yet more, and still yet more, with Him and for Him, that it seemed at last as if nothing short of the cross itself could satisfy her soul! And Jesus all the time stood there and watched her, satiating Himself, so to speak, with the loving longings of His little spouse, and when at last He was about to replace the heart of which He had so sweetly robbed her, He first sprinkled it with blood from His sacred side, and deigning graciously to assure her, that those precious crimson drops should be to Him as the seal whereby He had sealed it to Himself, to be united for ever to His own.

Marie's cousin stood by and watched her during the whole time that gracious visitation lasted, from morning even unto mid-day; and though the person of Our Divine Lord remained hidden from her eyes, she saw, and afterwards described minutely to Pere Albert, all the outward symptoms of His presence, of which I have already spoken—the rapture and fainting ecstacy, and almost dying state, into which it cast the invalid.

There were certain signs, in fact, accompanying almost all Marie's heavenly communications, which were not to be mistaken or passed over even by the commonest observer, for her face upon such occasions grew radiant as if bathed in the very light of heaven itself, her limbs became rigid in ecstacy as if made of marble, and the chamber in which she lay was suddenly filled with a perfume so indescribably delicious that Pere Albert, knowing no earthly flower possessed of such a fragrance, declared he could simply compare it to nothing less than an actual foretaste and enjoyment of the odors of Paradise—even the heavenly Eden of the saints of God!

Nor was this a passing fragrance; it lingered long hours afterwards, both about Marie's person, and throughout her humble dwelling, so that people who came to visit her could not help remarking it, or refrain from inquiring as to the nature of the perfume which she, so poor and self-deniant in all other matters, carried continually about her.

Some one, in alluding to it, once mentioned the scent of roses, and Marie, whom the subject humbled and distressed beyond measure, took the hint, and was careful ever afterwards to have a bouquet of those bright summer blossoms (whenever it was possible) in her room, in order to mislead the imaginations of her visitors. The ruse, however, was not always perfectly successful, for Pere Albert tells us this supernatural fragrance proceeded so evidently from her person, and was so unique and wonderful in its essence, that no one could for a moment mistake it for the breathings even of the rose—the sweetest of earth-born flowers, and queen and mistress of all the others.

In the midst of all these heavenly favors and visitations, the dying woman preserved herself in a humility which her director and biographer considered, and with reason, to have been even more wonderful than the very wonders themselves of which she was the object, and the seal, moreover, which was set upon them, to guarantee them genuine.

The nearer God approached her, the tenderer the caresses He lavished on her—the more sublime and continued the union with Himself to which He called her, the more thoroughly did she realize the fact of her own nothingness—the more profoundly did she humble herself beneath that knowledge, the more bitterly and incessantly did she bewail and punish those passing shades of imperfection, by which the saints themselves pay tribute to the weakness of their human origin.

God filled her with graces, because He knew her beforehand to be one of those chosen souls who would not rob Him of His glory, by attributing them as merit to themselves—He lifted her into the higher walks of sanctity, because He saw that she was ready and willing to remain, if He so willed it, even in the lowest—and He fed her with a foretaste of the joys of heaven, because, having abandoned all sensual gratifications, even the most innocent, for His sake, her hunger and thirst after those which were celestial became so keen as to demand, and almost to require, such heavenly nourishment continually at His hands. Even while receiving it, however, Marie never forgot that it was neither by raptures nor ecstacies that souls are saved, but by the constant exercise of all solid virtues, and chiefly of humility. So careful indeed was she to preserve the latter in the full beauty of its bloom, that though well aware of her approaching death, having more than once predicted it to Pere Albert, she would never allow the fatal nature of her illness to become known to her friends in general, hoping thus to depart this life without the distinction and possible damage to her soul which might have ensued from the numerous and ill-assorted visitors whom the news would certainly have gathered round her death-bed. When first she hinted to Pere Albert her conviction that she was soon to die, he could not, with all his faith in her prophetic powers, bring himself to believe her, for, as he himself ingenuously tells us, serious as he knew her malady to be, he had nevertheless so often seen her pass at once from the grasp of death to sudden and unexpected life, that he would have been taken far less by surprise by a miraculous recovery, than he was by her death when it actually occurred. Marie took no heed of his incredulity, but quietly commenced her more immediate preparations for death. This, thanks to the life which she had led for over sixty years, was neither a difficult nor unwelcome task.

Her first care was to destroy all those instruments of penance by which, for so many years, she had chastised her body, in the shape of chains, disciplines, and hair-shirts, and among the latter, that especial one, so terrible from its size and roughness, in which in times of extraordinary penance she had been accustomed to clothe herself from head to foot. All these she burned or otherwise put out of sight, acknowledging afterwards to Pere Albert that she had done so, knowing well that she would never again have health or strength to use them. Probably also she feared, though she did not say it, that he and some others of her friends, might take possession of them, and regard them with veneration as proofs of the spirit of penance, by which from first to last, her soul had been conducted, and to which, from first to last, she had ever rendered such a marvelous and prompt obedience.

Her next care was to deliver to her director a will which she had drawn up two years previously, without, however, having mentioned the fact to him at the time.

Having always lived from day to day by the labor of her own hands, she had of course little or nothing to leave to any one.

The dispositions of her will, therefore, were very simple, but either among them, or in her verbal instructions afterwards to the father, she made some provisions in favor of certain persons who were professedly her enemies.

Knowing how grievously they had sinned against her, Pere Albert could not resist a movement of annoyance and surprise, and he even ventured to remind her that these very persons had done their best to stigmatise her to the world as a busy-body and hypocrite. But Marie silenced him at once, answering, as the good father humbly acknowledges, with far more wisdom than he had spoken, "that she was astonished to hear him speak thus; as for her own part, she had always prayed very especially for them, and hoped to do so still more especially after her death, when, if she herself attained salvation, she would do all in her power to procure a similar boon for them."

In these few words are contained, in fact, the very essence of the sanctity whereby Marie sanctified her life.

Charity to all mankind, and even to her foes, had ever been the most conspicuous of her virtues, the fount and origin, as it were, from whence all the others flowed. Far more ready to forgive than any one would be to inflict injury upon her, she was often heard to say, (and the maxim is at once so practical and so sublime, it is worth inscribing here,) "that we should pardon our enemies and do good to those who hate us, not merely because God has made such forgiveness the condition of our own pardon, but also because, albeit it may be contrary to their actual intention, He will in that case make their evil dealings towards us a means whereby we may acquire for our souls such a measure of heroic virtue as will enable them, instead of walking or even running, to fly with strong steady wings rapidly in those high paths of sanctity which lead straight to Him."

After this last act of heroic sanctity in the pardon of her enemies, Marie's mission upon earth appeared to be fulfilled, and as Pere Albert watched her fading day by day and hour by hour almost visibly away, he began to feel at last that she was right in her predictions after all, and that this time, at all events, her illness was unto death.

On the feast of the Nativity of the Blessed Virgin, therefore, in the September of the year 1684, he allowed her to make the last and most important of all preparations for her journey, by the reception of the body and blood of Christ as its viaticum; holy communion, as well as extreme unction, being administered to her publicly, and with all due observance of ceremonial, by the Doyen Cure of the parish.

From that moment Marie became more than ever absorbed in the sufferings of her Divine Spouse, more than ever fixed and earnest in that last sublime desire of her soul, to live, as He had lived, without human comfort, and to die, as He had died, abandoned and alone,—her sole consolation in the thought that thus, in its measure and due degree, her death had been made somewhat resembling His. "Mon Pere," said the dying woman, with a quiet smile, when on the day before her death Pere Albert, seeing the grievous sufferings of body and soul of which she was the willing victim, asked if he could not procure her relief or consolation; "Mon Pere, I want no other consolation than the hope of dying, as my Beloved died, without comfort or consolation, on the cross."

Unable, however, out of the great tenderness of his heart to acquiesce entirely in this sentence of abandonment pronounced against herself, Pere Albert tried to put the matter on another footing, by inquiring if his own presence at her death-bed would not be a comfort to her.

"A comfort!" she answered, quickly, " yes, undoubtedly it would; but for that very reason it must not be."

"For that very reason it ought to be," he answered, earnestly.

But Marie could only repeat in thought and word, "He died alone! He died alone!" and not daring to interfere further, or to put his earthly presence between her and that great grace whereby, as it seemed to him, God had inspired her to reserve her last moments entirely for Himself, the good father reluctantly withdrew.

He returned, however, in the evening, and finding her apparently much in the same state in which he had left her a few hours before, he began to think that perhaps, after all, death was not so near as he had first supposed it to be.

Marie, however, felt that she was sinking fast, and told him so, showing in confirmation of the fact, her hands, which were greatly swollen. So was her face, in fact, as he remembered afterwards; though at the moment, God, willing perhaps to indulge his faithful spouse in the merits of that utter dereliction which she thus earnestly desired, so blinded the eyes and understanding of the good father, that the fatal nature of the symptom never even struck him; and when Marie spoke of going speedily, he fancied she merely meant that in all probability she could not hold out more than a few days longer. Even when, in reply to her cousin's request that she would take some cordial, she refused, with the observation, " that she would soon drink of a liquor more delicious than that in heaven," he did not take in the full meaning of the words. She was dying, in truth, before his very eyes, and he never even dreamed it.

A few minutes afterwards he departed, and Marie's cousin, who now usually returned to her own house at night, having also taken leave, the dying woman was left in the care of her young apprentices until morning. These were mostly girls whom she had rescued either from crime or the chances of being drawn into crime, and as they all loved her dearly, they watched over her during the long hours of the weary night as tenderly and devotedly as if she had been their mother. She suffered them to linger about her until early dawn, then telling them that she was well enough to be left alone, she bade them take some rest themselves.

At first they were unwilling to obey her, but as she seemed at last to be going off into a quiet slumber, they retreated, in order to content her, into their own little chamber, which was only separated from hers by a half partition made of wood.

Like Pere Albert, they were completely blinded as to her real state, and they fancied she was sleeping, whereas she was simply dying,—dying, as the saints die, in peace and unutterable tranquility. When in the morning they returned to wait upon her, they found her in the same attitude in which they had left her over night, her mouth and eyes calmly closed, and the crucifix in her hands. They thought at first that she was still sleeping quietly, and it was only on touching her that they discovered that she was dead.

Long years before, upon a certain feast of Pentecost, when she was only at the commencement of her career of sanctity, a dove, let loose, according to ancient custom, from the high altar of the collegiate church of Liege, after soaring once or twice uncertainly over the heads of the congregation, took refuge, calm and unruffled, upon Marie's bosom. Men thought it at the time prophetic of her future sanctity; it seems to me, at all events, that it may be considered as a graceful foreshadowing of that moment when, freed from the bonds of flesh, her soul, dove-like in its innocence and fearless beauty, soared upwards, never faltering or swerving in its flight until it had reached its eternal home—the home of all the saints—the bosom of its God.

Sœur Marie was interred in the church of the Carmelite fathers, close to the altar of St. Albert, before which, from childhood to old age, she had spent so many long hours in prayer; and upon the stone which marked the spot, Pere Albert caused this modest and unpretending inscription to be engraven :—

"Beneath this stone, rests in peace the body of our very dear sister, 'Marie Ock;' in religion, 'Sœur Marie Albert, of the cross of Jesus,' but commonly known as 'Marie Sellier,' tertiary of the order of the B. V. M. of Mount Carmel—deceased on the 13th of October 1684."

This church unhappily exists no longer! In the terrible days of the French Revolution, it was first desecrated, and then destroyed, and a vast multitude of incongruous buildings have since been gradually erected upon the site which it occupied.

The tomb of Sœur Marie has consequently disappeared, and will never be honored by the veneration of the faithful, but albeit this external evidence of her existence has been destroyed, her memory still floats like a good odor of virtue through the streets of Liege! While its rich men and magistrates have passed away, without leaving even a record of their lives behind them, their titles of nobility, and their very names forgotten, that of

Marie Sellier, the saddler's daughter, is still cherished as a household word. People visit such of the old churches as time and the wickedness of man have spared, and say to themselves, "It was here that she often prayed," or they wander through the oldest and most forlorn portion of their city, whispering as they go, "It was in these wretched purlieus that she spent her days, seeking out and solacing the poor!"

For so it is, and so it ever will be! Men who have lived for themselves, and their own selfish interests only, however wealthy they may have been, or however noble; when they die, are either forgotten altogether, or remembered only for their wickedness; while those who, even in the obscurity of humble life, have contrived, by their unselfish charities, to make themselves almoners, as it were, to the whole human race, descend to the grave indeed, but not most assuredly to oblivion. Centuries pass away, and their names are remembered still; and their actions still, to quote once more the often quoted words of the poet--

"Smell sweet and blossom in the dust."

THE END.

www.ingramcontent.com/pod-product-compliance
Lightning Source LLC
Chambersburg PA
CBHW020824230426
43666CB00007B/1090